100 Horses in History

100 Horses in History

TRUE STORIES OF HORSES WHO SHAPED OUR WORLD

Gayle Stewart

Library of Congress Control Number: 2015932009

ISBN 978-0-692-17219-3

Printed in the United States
Second Edition: 2018

Contents

Dedication

For Rob and Wyatt, who make my life such fun.

1 TRAILBLAZERS

These horses boasted traits so unique that some founded new breeds, while others set lofty standards for their descendants.

Eohippus

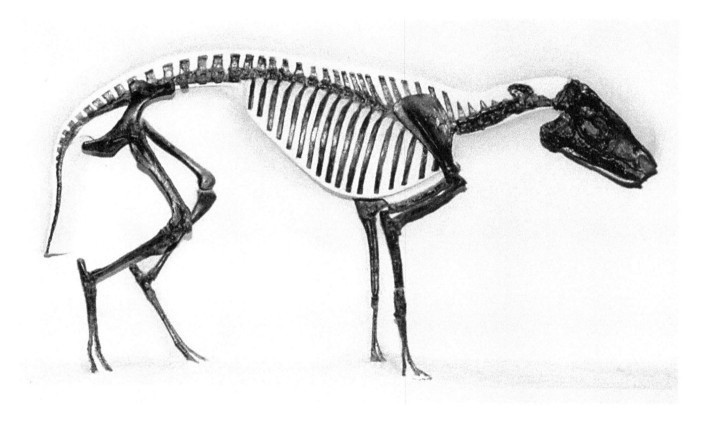

This little guy, an ancestor of today's modern horse, roamed swampland and subtropical forests during the early Eocene Epoch, about fifty-five to fifty million years ago.

Standing only about ten to seventeen inches tall at the shoulder, with a length of about two feet, he had four hoofed toes in front and three hoofed toes behind. His front legs were shorter than his hind legs, so he bobbed up and down as he browsed for soft leaves and plant shoots. As millennia passed, Eohippus's future relatives developed one toe…a single hoof!

Skeletal fragments of this timid creature were found in Kent, England, and "described" (named) in 1841 by Sir Richard Owen as *Hyracotherium*. In 1876, Yale University professor O.C. Marsh described jaw fragments found in North America from the same species as Eohippus. The word Eohippus derives from the Greek "eos," meaning dawn, and "hippos," meaning horse; thus the "dawn horse" of recent life.

Eohippus fossils have been found in the Wasatch Range of Utah and the Wind River Basin in Wyoming.

Eohippus was an early ancestor of today's modern horse.

The Darley Arabian

At the very turn of the eighteenth century, among a Bedouin tribe wandering the sweltering sands of the Syrian Desert, a bay colt was born who would change history. He was the second of the three Thoroughbred foundation sires to arrive in England.

"I believe he will not be much disliked."

These prophetic words, written by Thomas Darley to his brother, Richard, on December 21, 1703, sealed the directive from their father: Buy an Arabian stallion for breeding at the family seat, Aldby Park, near Yorkshire in northern England.

Darley, a British diplomat and merchant working in Syria, somehow persuaded Sheikh Mirza II to sell this favored foal.

"…he has a blaze downe his face, something of the largest. He is about fifteen hands high, of the most esteemed race among the Arabs, both by Syre and Dam, and the name of the said race is called Mannicka."

The colt arrived at Aldby Park, where he lived out his life, and thereafter was called the Darley Arabian. Though he fathered few foals, his descendants include a Who's Who of famous Thoroughbreds: Flying Childers, Eclipse, Sir Barton, Secretariat, Affirmed, and Seattle Slew.

His male descendants helped establish new breeds: Messenger, a foundation sire of the American Standardbred; Manica, a foundation sire of the Cleveland Bay; and Old Shales, a foundation sire of the Hackney.

The Darley Arabian died in 1730 at an elderly thirty years old.

The Darley Arabian

The Byerley Turk

After more than 300 years, mystery still shrouds the ancestry of the Byerley Turk, the earliest of the three Thoroughbred foundation stallions (joined later by the Darley Arabian and the Godolphin Arabian). Where was the beautiful bay stallion born and how did he come to live in England?

An early theory says he was captured by British officer Captain Robert Byerley at the siege of Vienna in 1683. John Evelyn, an English diarist, wrote on September 23, 1684, of seeing three "Turkes or Asian Horses," newly arrived by ship in London's St. James Park.

The Byerley Turk

"They trotted like does as if they did not feel the ground… It was judged by the spectators among whom was the King, the Prince of Denmark, Duke of Yorke and several of the Court, noble persons skill'd in horses…that there were never seene any horses in these parts to be compar'd with them."

Another theory places Captain Byerley, a rising star in the cavalry of King William III of Orange, in Hungary in 1686. The English had defeated the Turks of the Ottoman Empire in the Battle of Buda; Captain Byerley noticed a fiery, dark-bay stallion ridden by an enemy officer and took him home, arriving in England in 1688.

In 1689, now-Colonel Byerley's regiment was engaged in another war waged by King William, this one over religion. King William, a Dutch Protestant, had dethroned British King James II, who ruled Ireland as a Roman Catholic.

King James wanted his throne back and rallied Irishmen to help him fight the mighty British. Colonel Byerley led the British troops and in July 1690, during the Battle of the Boyne, the stallion saved Byerley's life. Enemy cavalry encircled them, poised to capture or kill. Undaunted, Byerley and the horse who had become famous as the "Byerley Turk" outmaneuvered the Irish soldiers and led England to victory. Byerley's stallion was so strong, handsome, and fast that

Goldsborough Hall, North Yorkshire

admiring British officers dubbed him "Byerley's Treasure."

A new theory about the Byerley Turk's origins has surfaced in research by Dr. Richard Nash, professor of English at Indiana University. Nash found no evidence that Captain Byerley ever served in Hungary, so Byerley could not have acquired the horse there. But it is certain that Byerley rode him in the Battle of the Boyne.

Nash says the stallion was born in England and inherited by Mary Wharton, the granddaughter of Sir Richard Hutton, owner of Goldsborough Hall, the family estate in North Yorkshire. She also inherited Goldsborough Hall. So Byerley, according to Nash, inherited the horse and the estate as Mary Wharton's guardian in 1685. When she grew up, Mary married Robert Byerley!

We know one thing for sure: the Byerley Turk was a spectacular and talented stallion whose bloodline flourished, primarily through his son Jigg and outstanding daughters. The Turk was the grandsire of Partner — "the best racehorse of his day" — and was the great-great grandsire of Herod and the great-great-great grandsire of Highflyer, a Herod son. Highflyer's success as a sire provided his owner, Richard Tattersall, the funds to establish the British company which operates the famous Newmarket horse sales.

The Byerley Turk retired at Goldsborough Hall and died in 1706 at about age twenty-six. He was buried on the grounds of Goldsborough Hall, having lived a long, illustrious life, no doubt due to the finest care.

The Godolphin Arabian

The Godolphin Arabian

The passage of time can dim even the most stellar reputation. Great personalities lose their due and are forgotten.

Not so with the Godolphin Arabian, who lives forever in the bloodlines he passed on in the course of nearly three centuries. He was the last of the three Thoroughbred foundation sires to come to England.

Standing about 14.2 hands, he was a dark bay-brown and boasted bright eyes, a broad forehead, and a massive, arched neck. He sired only about ninety foals.

Born in 1724 in southern Arabia, he arrived at the royal stables of the Bey (chieftain) of Tunis and named Sham. In a gesture of friendship, the Bey gifted four of his finest stallions to the king of France, Louis XV. The long ocean voyage nearly killed them and all arrived in pitiful condition. Even so, the French aristocrat Vicomte de Manty described Sham as "a horse of incomparable beauty whose only flaw was being headstrong."

The king (thinking them small) did not keep them. He turned three loose in the forests of Brittany. The fourth, Sham, was imported to England by Edward Coke in 1729. When Coke died, Sham was bequeathed to Roger Williams and then sold to the second Earl of Godolphin in Cambridgeshire, where he lived the rest of his life.

Now called the Godolphin Arabian, he and the mare Roxana in 1732 produced a fine colt named Lath, "the best racehorse of his day;" Cade in 1733, founder of the Matchem line; and Regulus in 1739. Regulus never lost a race and sired a mare named Spiletti, dam of Eclipse. Another famous Godolphin descendant was Man o' War.

The Godolphin Arabian died on Christmas Day 1753 at the Earl's Gog Magog Stable at age twenty-nine. He was buried under the stable gateway.

Blaze

A stolen mare's chance encounter with a stallion in northern England produced a founding father of a new breed of hearty and handsome draft horses.

By the time she was returned to her rightful owner in Scotland, she carried within her a foal sired by a big Flemish stallion. Her black colt, born in 1778, boasted blue-ribbon looks from the start. A wide white stripe ran down his face, "feathered" white hair frilled his legs, and white socks (resembling a school girl's knee-highs) festooned each leg. His owner named him Blaze.

In 1784, Blaze won first prize in the Grass Market stallion show in Edinburgh. Over the twenty-two years of his life, Blaze stamped his foals with strength, good looks, and intelligence.

These gentle giants, sired by Blaze and others, began to be called Clydesdales because they first flourished in Lanarkshire; Clydesdale is the old name of the district. They toiled in farmers' fields as haulers of heavy loads and carriages, and in war.

Scottish author Sir Walter Scott wrote in his novel *Fair Maid of Perth* of a bonnet maker and a Clydesdale: "The saddle and the man were girthed on the ridged bone of a great trampling Flemish mare, with a nose turned up in the air like a camel, a huge fleece of hair at each foot, and every hoof full as large in circumference as a frying-pan. The contrast between the beast and the rider was so extremely extraordinary, that, whilst chance passengers contented themselves with wondering how he got up, his friends were anticipating with sorrow the perils which must attend his coming down again."

A stylish Scot, the Clydesdale steps high and gracefully as he trots gaily along, as if keeping time to the skirl of a Scottish bagpipe.

Prince Cedric III, a classic Clydesdale stallion

Eclipse

Eclipse

When the duke died the year after Eclipse was born, the colt was sold to businessman William Wildman. Eclipse proved difficult to handle and was not raced until May 3, 1769, when he was five years old.

Watching the Epsom races that day was Irish gambler Dennis O'Kelly, and Eclipse caught his eye. After Eclipse won the first of his three four-mile heats, O'Kelly predicted: "Eclipse first, the rest nowhere." (In that era, horses running 240 yards behind the leader were described as "nowhere.")

O'Kelly was right: Eclipse won all three races. Determined to own Eclipse, O'Kelly wrangled a half-share from Wildman for 650 guineas, then in 1770 purchased the second half for 1,100 guineas.

Eclipse won all twenty-six of his races and sired 344 winners and three Epsom Derby winners: Young Eclipse, Saltram, and Sergeant. An important descendant was St. Simon, an undefeated stallion who won the 1884 Ascot Cup by twenty lengths and was one of England's most successful sires.

Two celestial phenomena struck on April 1, 1764 — one in the heavens and one in the barn.

A fiery chestnut colt was born during the great solar eclipse that day, coming into the world with a royal breeder, royal ancestors, and a royal temper.

Bred by the Duke of Cumberland and named for the astronomical rarity, Eclipse was in the male line of the Darley Arabian and related to the Godolphin Arabian through his dam, Spiletta.

Pluto

The Lipizzan breed is one of the oldest in the world, favored and nurtured for hundreds of years by Austrian royalty, beginning in 1580 with Archduke Karl II. Hoping to upgrade the horses in his stable, he crossed Spanish horses with various bloodlines, including Arabians, at the Imperial Stud in Lipizza, near the Adriatic Sea. The breed was born and flourished.

About 150 years later, Emperor of Habsburg Karl VI — proud of his Lipizzans and wanting to show them off — began construction on the Winter Riding School in Vienna. The hall, as grand as the Hofburg Palace it adjoins, features marble columns, balconies, and crystal chandeliers that sparkle in the sunshine flooding through the windows.

In this magnificent setting, traditions of the Spanish Riding School carry on today as they did during Karl VI's reign. Master trainers of the Spanish Riding School teach riders and Lipizzan stallions the secrets and skills of the ancient classical art of equitation — "haute école." With a ballet dancer's precision, the Lipizzans trot to a polka and Mozart symphony, and execute the pas de deux, quadrille, and the piaffe. Only the bravest and strongest stallions perform the spectacular "Airs Above the Ground," skills originally taught as military maneuvers to deal swift and surprising blows to enemies.

These maneuvers include the capriole: the Lipizzan leaps through the air then kicks out behind; the levade: he balances on his hind legs for several seconds at a thirty-degree angle; and the courbette: starting from the levade, he hops forward several times on back legs, forelegs held high.

In 1765, thirty years after the Winter Riding School was completed, Pluto, the first of the foundation sires of the Lipizzan breed, was born. He grew up, as might a prince, at the Castle of Fredericksborg in Denmark, the Danish royal family's summer residence. In 1772, Pluto and five mares from the Danish Stud were sent to Lipizza, and Pluto established his dynasty.

"And the Lipizzaner!" praised Alois Podhajsky, former Spanish Riding School director. "These proud and noble white stallions! Their high intelligence and exceptional talent are already obvious during training. It is a pleasure to work with these clever horses, and it is easy to understand why the great masters of the Spanish Riding School are so passionately devoted to them and so full of praise for their qualities."

In 1919 and several wars later, the Imperial Stud was moved to Piber in the Austrian Alps, where Lipizzan foals and mares run freely, grazing on mountain pastures, cavorting in winter snows. Only stallions train in Vienna and not until they are four.

Lipizzans boast the grace of a ballerina, the power of engine pistons, beauty, keen intelligence, and above all, courage — thanks to Pluto and the sires who followed him: Conversano, Maestoso, Favory, Neapolitano, and Siglavy.

Morning Exercise in the Hofreitschule, Josephsplatz, 1890

Justin Morgan

A little bay colt named Figure and George Washington shared destinies as patriarchs of their own First Families.

In 1789, Washington was elected the first president of the United States, and a foal born in southern New England grew up to father the first American horse breed: the Morgan.

Justin Morgan, the man, lived and worked as a singing master and schoolteacher in Randolph, Vermont, not long after America became a nation. In 1792, Morgan walked all the way from his home to West Springfield, Massachusetts, to collect a debt. But his debtor had no money and, to settle up, instead gave Morgan two horses — one large, older horse; the second, a bay colt. Morgan easily sold the older horse, but nobody wanted the colt. He seemed too small to do much heavy work in Vermont's Green Mountains. So Morgan kept him and named him Figure, not imagining he would become a famous stallion known by his owner's name — Justin Morgan — and would stamp his future progeny with traits still seen today.

Figure looked delicate yet stout. He was smallish and bull-strong with muscled hindquarters, a short and strong back, and a pleasant personality. Wide-set and expressive eyes, dainty ears, and a high-crested neck complemented his hardiness. He was a tiger in competition.

"…a horse that was right every way under the heavens and would go very fast; an awful good horse," praised Solomon Yurann, a Vermonter who knew Figure.

He was ridden, driven, and raced; hauled freight; and pulled logs. In about 1796, he won $50 in a race in Brookfield, Vermont, in which he beat New York racehorses Sweepstakes and Silvertail. The site of that race is known today as "Morgan's Mile."

In 1804, he won a "pulling bee" at General Butler's Tavern in St. Johnsbury, Vermont. On July 22, 1817, Figure proudly carried President James Monroe in a parade in Montpelier, Vermont.

He sired many foals, stamping them and future generations with his personal seal of intelligence, stamina, athleticism, and beauty. He lived to be thirty-two years old, having had many owners and names, including the Justin, the Justin Morgan horse, and just Justin Morgan.

He was the little horse who could.

Justin Morgan founded a new breed.

Gaines' Denmark 61

I n the mid-1880s, a keen-eyed Kentuckian and a beautiful black stallion forged a partnership that influences the American Saddlebred even today.

Though the Thoroughbred Denmark F. S. is the designated foundation sire of the American Saddlebred, most consider his son, Gaines' Denmark 61, to be the real progenitor of the breed.

Born in 1851, the black stallion was bred by William V. Cromwell and originally known as Black Diamond. E. P. Gaines of Scott County, Kentucky, purchased him for $1,000 in his three-year-old year. At the time it was thought to be the highest price ever paid for a Kentucky Saddler, precursor to the breed as we know it today. The stallion became known as Gaines' Denmark and was eventually given the registration number 61.

Unfortunately, Gaines' Denmark also caught the eye of the Confederate army. The American Civil War was raging, and horses of all types, talents, and ownership were conscripted into service by the North and South — the Union Army and the Confederate States of America. Gaines' treasured stallion served for two years in the southern command of Brigadier General John Hunt Morgan. As did most cavalry horses, he suffered from lack of food, proper care, and long hours under saddle.

Gaines' Denmark 61

By good fortune, one day Gaines recognized his stallion, though in pitiful condition, among the cavalry horses. He hurriedly traded for him, and Gaines' Denmark returned home to good food and care. Gaines' Denmark recovered and lived to be fifteen years old.

Almost all registered American Saddlebreds trace to Denmark F. S., the majority through his son Gaines' Denmark 61. More than 60 percent of the horses listed in the American Saddlebred Horse Association's first three registries trace to Gaines' Denmark 61.

The American Saddlebred is championed as a show horse, spectacular under the bright lights of stakes nights, especially when the five-gaited Saddlebred performs at the slow gait or rack. The ability of the five-gaited horse to perform these lateral gaits is inherited from his ancestors, the Narragansett Pacers.

Yet the Saddlebred, whose bright eye reflects intelligence, kindness, and an eagerness to please, is multi-talented and performs with pride in many disciplines, including dressage, jumping, as a field hunter, and on trail rides.

So the next time you see an American Saddlebred at work, teaching a timid child to ride, or enjoying family life as a backyard pet — remember Gaines' Denmark 61, his sire Denmark F. S., and a man named Gaines, whose vision gave us the American Saddlebred we know today.

Wimpy P-1

A chestnut stallion born on the legendary King Ranch© in South Texas — and given the unlikely name of Wimpy — holds a revered place in Quarter Horse history as the first stallion registered in the stud book of the American Quarter Horse Association. He earned the honor at the 1941 Southwestern Exposition and Fat Stock Show in Fort Worth, Texas, by winning the grand champion stallion halter class.

The winning stallion, decided the newly formed AQHA, would be awarded the designation "P-1," meaning "permanent" registration number 1.

Winning the championship was prestigious beyond measure. At stake were forever bragging rights, and ranch president Bob Kleberg, Jr., wanted to enter one of his stout, smart, and good working stallions. After consulting with ranch cow horse foreman Lauro Cavazos and veterinarian Dr. J. K. Northway, he selected Wimpy.

"…there was a sizable crowd on hand," reported Frank Reeves in the Fort Worth *Star-Telegram* (March 14, 1941), "and before all halter classes were completed at noon one of the largest crowds ever assembled for a horse event was present.

"(Wimpy), owned by the King Ranch, Kingsville, was the winner of the class for stallions 3 years old and over, and then went on to win the championship in competition with Jim Dandy, owned by Elmer Hepler, of Carlsbad, N.M., winner of the class for 2-year-old stallions."

Wimpy P-1 was the first stallion registered in the American Quarter Horse Association.

Wimpy was born in 1937, a son of Solis and the mare Panda, and the grandson of Old Sorrel, a King Ranch foundation sire. In 1958, when Wimpy was twenty-one, the ranch gave him to George Clegg of Alice, Texas, the breeder of Old Sorrel.

Later, Clegg sold him to Rex Cauble of Crockett, Texas. On August 13, 1959, Wimpy died and is buried in Crockett.

Ranch lore suggests that Wimpy might have been named by an employee who compared his ravenous appetite to the cravings of hamburger-munching J. Wellington Wimpy, a character in Popeye cartoons.

Wimpy P-1 sired 174 registered Quarter Horses and was inducted into the American Quarter Horse Association Hall of Fame in 1989. His bronze statue welcomes visitors to AQHA's international headquarters in Amarillo, Texas.

Hambletonian 10

The foundation sire of the American Standardbred — the "trotting horse" — was a muscular bay named Hambletonian 10.

He was born on May 5, 1849, in Sugar Loaf, New York, a great-grandson of the imported English Thoroughbred stallion Messenger and son of the stallion Abdallah.

Another son of Abdallah, Abdallah Chief, was a keen rival of Hambletonian. They raced each other, with their owners driving, in 1852 at Union Course on Long Island. Hambletonian beat Abdallah Chief to the finish line. But the owner of Abdallah Chief was convinced he owned the better stallion and hoped to prove it. In the only time trial of his career, Hambletonian trotted the mile in 2:48½; Abdallah Chief's time was 2:55½.

A New Yorker named Jonas Seeley originally owned Hambletonian and his dam. But William Rysdyk, an employee of Seeley who cared for and loved the two, convinced Seeley to sell the pair for $125.

Hambletonian sired 1,331 foals and founded the American Standardbred, his bloodline the only viable Standardbred bloodline to survive. He died at age twenty-seven on March 27, 1876, and he and Rysdyk

Hambletonian 10

(who died in 1870) were buried in Chester, New York.

In 1893, thanks to funds raised by his fans, a granite monument was placed on Hambletonian's grave on Hambletonian Avenue. He was inducted into the Harness Racing Museum's Hall of Immortals in 1953.

The Hambletonian is an annual, one-mile race for three-year-old trotters and is harness racing's most-prestigious event.

Creation's King

England's first version of the "ultimate driving machine" boasted hooves and tails rather than headlights and tires. Decades before automobiles hogged the road, the stylish and swift Hackney horse and pony swept the country.

The English began crossing their fast Norfolk Trotters with grandsons of Thoroughbred foundation stallions and were delighted with the result. The first Hackney (as we know the breed today) was a horse named The Shale's Horse, born in 1760.

Hackney horses — soon followed by Hackney ponies — squired English gentry along London's boulevards and English country roads, moving fast and stepping high. As English roads improved, big, heavy draft horses no longer were needed. A shiny carriage pulled by a Hackney offered perfect conveyance for elegant travel.

In the mid-1800s, wealthy American railroad magnate A. J. Cassatt visited England and was smitten with the Hackney. In 1878 he imported to Philadelphia, Pennsylvania, the first Hackney pony, a pretty

mare named 239 Stella. Soon boatloads of Hackney horses and ponies sailed the Atlantic from England to American shores, and both countries gloried in their Hackneys during the "Golden Age of Driving."

In America a Hackney pony stallion named Creation's King established himself as a foundation sire. Born in 1939, a son of King of the Highlands and the mare Penwortham Creation, he sired more than 200 foals.

Cassatt and other lovers of the Hackney — "the high stepping aristocrat of the show ring" — founded the American Hackney Horse Society in 1891.

Creation's King

Dawndee

Dawndee was a working mother of the 1960s, nursing a newborn, then leaving home to work a day job. She was born in Utah in 1959, a pretty Appaloosa filly. A white blanket with dark spots draped her hindquarters. Glade and Isabel Draper of Santoquin, Utah, bred, owned, and trained her.

In 1961, she was bred to the Quarter Horse stallion War Glory, a descendant of Man o' War. Dawndee raced during the pregnancy, delivered in April, went back to work on the racetrack, then returned to the barn to nurse her foal — a colt named War Don.

She excelled at everything. Dawndee placed second in the 1961 Utah State Junior Livestock Show, competing in a large halter class of two year olds. That year she won the 250-yard race at the Panguitch race meet by almost a length, carrying 135 pounds and besting competition which included Thoroughbreds and Quarter Horses carrying less weight. As an aged mare of eight, Dawndee set an Appaloosa Horse Club world record, running 640 yards in 33.4 seconds. She won four of seven starts in her final year of racing.

War Don, emulating his mother, retiring with a race record of 16-10-1-1 and earned a spot in the Appaloosa Horse Club Racing Hall of Fame in 1988. He sired champion racehorses War Reed, War Belle, and War

Dawndee

Don's Darling. From his bloodline descend many good runners.

Pay N Go was a star among Dawndee's descendants. The 1984 gelding competed at the Grand Prix dressage level and performed at the 1998 memorial service for Appaloosa lover Linda McCartney (late wife of former Beatle, Sir Paul McCartney).

Dawndee died in 1990 at age thirty-one and entered the Appaloosa Horse Club Racing Hall of Fame in 1995.

Old Billy

The *Guinness Book of World Records* bills Old Billy as the world's longest-living horse — sixty-two years. The big horse, probably a Cleveland Bay cross, was born in 1760 and bred by Edward Robinson of Wild Grave Farm in Woolston, Lancashire, England.

When he was two or three, the Mersey and Irwell Navigation Company bought Old Billy (maybe he was just called Billy then) to work as a "gin horse." Working from the river bank, he pulled a hoist that moved heavy loads onto and off of barges and boats plying the canals and waterways of the rivers Mersey and Irwell. The company also stationed Old Billy, utilizing his strength and good sense, riverside to tow boats needing extra power to reach their final destinations of either the Irish Sea or port.

Old Billy lived to be sixty-two years old.

Old Billy toiled decade after decade and, until about age fifty, had "an extremely vicious disposition, not only to human beings but to dogs or any other animals that happened to oppose his progress, or stand in his way…particularly at the dinner hour…"

He used "very savagely, either his heels or teeth (particularly the latter) to remove any living impediment, whether pig, dog or child…"

At age fifty-nine, Old Billy found sweet retirement on a farm in Warrington.

Old Billy's long life spanned world-changing events including the American Revolution (1775–1783); British Captain James Cook's landing on the Sandwich Islands, now Hawaii (1778); the Napoleonic Wars (1799–1815), and the coronations of British Kings George III and George IV (1760 and 1820). Old Billy died on November 27, 1822, three years into retirement.

The Manchester Museum at the University of Manchester in England showcases his mounted head; remarkable are his cropped ears, common among work horses in those days.

2 MOVIES, MUSIC, AND TIMELESS TALES

These horses and ponies inspired songs, starred in tales of daring adventures, and taught lessons in the kind treatment of animals.

Occident

Occident starred in early motion pictures.

O ccident should win an Academy Award. Posthumously, of course. His work of more than a century ago laid the groundwork for the creation of motion pictures.

A celebrated trotter, Occident was owned by Leland Stanford, an industrialist and politician who founded Stanford University. Stanford theorized that when a horse trots at one point all its feet are simultaneously off the ground. In 1872, he hired British photographer Eadweard Muybridge to prove his theory.

Muybridge photographed Occident trotting, pulling a sulky. The resulting photo was unsatisfactorily fuzzy.

In 1877, Muybridge published a new image of Occident. He used a painting of Occident trotting and a photo of the driver, then photographed the composition. The collage, labeled "Occident" Trotting at a 2:30 Gait, proved true Stanford's theory.

Taking the project farther, Muybridge built a photo studio at Stanford's California farm. Placing twelve cameras twenty-one inches apart and white sheets across the ground, he photographed Stanford's horses pulling sulkies and galloping under saddle. As the horses crossed the sheets, they tripped wires that fired super-fast shutters. These first stop-action photos were published in The Horse In Motion card series. Other Stanford horses photographed included Sallie Gardner, Abe Edgington, Mahomet, and Daisy.

In 1879 Muybridge invented a motion-picture projector called a zoopraxiscope. The zoopraxiscope rotated painted images on a glass disc — including horses — which simulated movement and gave life to the new art form of cinematography.

The Tennessee Stud

The "Tennessee Stud" was a horse owned by Jess Goodman, the grandfather of songwriter Jimmie Driftwood's wife, Cleda. Driftwood's 1958 song combined tales of two generations of Cleda's family: Goodman and John Merriman, her great-grandfather.

Much of the song describes Merriman's adventures during the early 1820s. Jess Goodman fought in the Civil War for the Union and when he got home to Tennessee, he found it unfriendly to Yankee sympathizers. He moved to Arkansas and founded the town of Timbo.

"He raised horses and raced them for money until the legislature outlawed it. When he went back to Tennessee, he found a girl, 'whupped her brother and whupped her pa' and brought her back to Arkansas. And when they got back home, it wasn't long before there was a pretty little horse colt in the yard and a little baby," Driftwood said.

Driftwood lived a long and prolific life, dying in 1998 at age ninety-one, having written about 6,000 songs. "Tennessee Stud" has been recorded many times, the first in 1959 by Eddy Arnold. That version reached No. 5 on the country music charts.

The "Tennessee Stud" song was based on true stories.

Rocinante

Rocinante was a skinny, old horse; Don Quixote, a middle-aged dreamer. But Don Quixote fancied himself a knight-errant in search of chivalry and his horse a young, proud steed.

In Spanish, Rocinante translates from "rocin," meaning "nag;" and "ante," meaning "before." So in Quixote's mind his horse used to be a nag.

Don Quixote, the hero of the novel *Don Quixote de La Mancha*, lived in Spain and loved to read stories of knights in shining armor. He imagined a peasant woman to be a beautiful woman named Dulcinea del Toboso. As a chivalrous knight, he decided he must disenchant her from a magic spell. Saving Dulcinea was his primary quest as he set out on Rocinante to right all wrongs he could find. Trailing behind Rocinante and Don Quixote was Sancho Panza, his "squire," riding his donkey Dapple.

Rocinante trod slowly, a faithful companion trying to please. On their journey, he chased romance of his own and some mares grazing nearby, only to be beaten by their owners and left lying in the road. Sancho helped Rocinante to his feet and Don Quixote onto Dapple's back. They rode on to an inn which the knight-errant mistook for a castle.

Another delusion of Don Quixote's forced Rocinante to charge a field of windmills, his master thinking the windmills were giants that needed slaying. This folly gave English the phrase — "tilting at windmills" — meaning to fight imaginary foes. (Tilting, in this instance, means jousting or using a lance.) Don Quixote also gave the English language the word "quixotic," meaning unrealistic or romantic.

Their adventures over, Rocinante carried Don Quixote home, his quest to find Dulcinea a failure.

Don Quixote and Rocinante tilt at windmills.

Lady Suffolk

Lady Suffolk

How could the spectacular Lady Suffolk inspire the folk song "The Old Gray Mare," which opens with: "Oh, the Old Gray mare, She ain't what she used to be…"?

Maybe she did, perhaps not. Trotting horse lore insists the song is about the lovely gray mare with a flowing tail. Some scholars think the song is based on "Old Gray Horse," first published in 1858, three years after Lady Suffolk died; others say it evolved from an Old South spiritual.

In any case, she was a star on the racetrack, setting world records and consistently beating the boys in her races. Born in 1833 in Smithtown, New York, she was a great-granddaughter of the Standardbred foundation sire Messenger.

On October 18, 1845, at the Beacon Course in Hoboken, New Jersey, Lady Suffolk accomplished what the late Philip A. Pines, long-time director of the Harness Racing Museum & Hall of Fame, said was the trotting sport's "equivalent of breaking the sound barrier." At age twelve, to sulky in single harness, she was the first 2:30 trotter (trotting a mile in 2:30 or less) and set a world record.

Her early life was far from glamorous. At about two, Lady Suffolk pulled a butcher/oyster cart around Smithtown. At four, showing signs of style and class, she caught the eye of liveryman David Bryan. He bought her and hired her out on occasion, then realized he had a speedster on his hands. He trained her to trot for the track.

Lady Suffolk — the "Queen of the Turf" — raced for sixteen seasons and won eighty-nine of 162 races…more than half! She set records under saddle, to wagon, and high-wheeled sulky. She died at age twenty-two in Vermont and was inducted into the Harness Racing Hall of Fame in 1967.

Trigger and Buttermilk

Roy Rogers and Trigger, "The Smartest Horse in the Movies"

T rigger and Buttermilk teamed together like pork-and-beans, peanut butter-and-jelly, and Roy and Dale.

They were the famous horses of the famous Western singing stars of movies and television — Roy Rogers and Dale Evans. During the 1950s and beyond in reruns, Roy and Dale entertained millions of baby boomers and their parents in *The Roy Rogers Show* — marking the trail to good and honest lives.

Trigger and Roy's Western-movie partnership began in the late 1930s and ran full-tilt through the 1940s. Then Dale joined the team and the first TV episode of The Roy Rogers Show aired in December 1951.

Trigger headlined in parades and special appearances, at fundraisers and birthday parties. Roy — billed as "King of the Cowboys" — attributed much of his success to Trigger — "The Smartest Horse in the Movies."

"If there hadn't been a Trigger, there probably wouldn't have been a Roy Rogers," he said.

The golden Palomino stallion, who was half Thoroughbred, knew dozens of tricks. He could sprint like a racehorse, slide to spectacular dust-raising stops, rear, sit like a dog, bow, dance, nod, kiss, count to twenty, and cover Roy with a blanket. He often received more than 25,000 fan letters a year.

Trigger was a star, he knew it, and was not above stealing scenes from his co-star. Roy just blamed "the ham in that horse." A smiling Roy atop a rearing Trigger graced the cover of Life magazine on July 12, 1943, and provided a feel-good break for America as it fought in World War II.

As is common in show business, Trigger and Roy adopted their names. Trigger started life as Golden Cloud. Roy was born Leonard Slye in Ohio.

Roy bought Trigger in 1938 for $2,500 from a Hollywood stable that leased movie horses. Roy's movie sidekick, Smiley Burnette, remarked that he was fast and quick — quick-on-the-trigger. So Roy named him Trigger.

"All those years he never once fell with me," Roy recalled. "He could spin on a dime and give you nine cents change." Trigger starred with Roy in 100 Roy Rogers Show episodes and eighty-eight films, and retired in 1957 at age twenty-five. He lived out his life happily at pasture and died at age thirty-three.

Earning a high Hollywood honor, Trigger's hoofprints, and Roy's boot and handprints were cast April 21, 1949, in the forecourt of Grauman's Chinese Theatre in Hollywood, California.

Buttermilk made his own smooth transition to Hollywood life. Legendary horse trainer Glenn Randall (who also trained Trigger) found the buckskin gelding working cattle on a ranch in Angora, Nebraska, in 1952. He was a handsome and handy little Quarter Horse, boasting black mane, tail, and legs, and starred in the television series. Dale named him Buttermilk, and they forged many happy trails with Roy and Trigger. He lived to be thirty-one.

Buttermilk, the favorite horse of "The Queen of the West"

Silver

"The Lone Ranger — A fiery horse with the speed of light, a cloud of dust, and a hearty Hi Yo, Silver!" and away thundered Silver into another episode of *The Lone Ranger*.

Silver partnered with the Lone Ranger to chase down the bad guys, save the ranch, fight injustice in the Wild West. The white stallion starred in Lone Ranger movies, film serials, personal appearances, comic books, and on television.

Silver was smart, athletic, and snow-goose white. His silver horseshoes and silver-studded saddle glistened in the sunshine.

Silver and the Lone Ranger

The Lone Ranger adventures began when Texas Rangers were trailing the Butch Cavendish gang. Betrayed by a guide, the patrol was ambushed and all the rangers were killed, including Captain Dan Reid. Or so the gang thought. Left for dead was the captain's younger brother. A childhood friend, the Native American Tonto, found young Reid barely alive and nursed him with wise Indian ways. Tonto told him he was the "lone" ranger left.

The ranger made a mask from his dead brother's black vest and vowed to conceal his identity as he righted wrongs wherever he found them. The Masked Man wore a white hat and shot silver bullets…never aiming to kill. Tonto, on his pinto horse Scout, rode at his side.

They caught the Cavendish gang, all except Butch himself. Staging another ambush, Butch shot and killed the Lone Ranger's horse.

Suddenly a hero without a horse, he and Tonto loaded their gear onto Scout and walked toward Wild Horse Valley. There, they'd heard, lived a powerful white stallion. Arriving at the valley, they found under way a grisly fight between the stallion and a buffalo, and the stallion was losing.

The Lone Ranger shot the buffalo and nursed the stallion, just as Tonto had nursed him. The stallion never forgot his kindness and served the Lone Ranger forever after.

Clayton Moore and John Hart played the Lone Ranger on television and in the movies. Jay Silverheels played Tonto alongside Moore's Lone Ranger. Several horses played the role of Silver. Two horses worked with Moore, including a Tennessee Walking Horse stallion named White Cloud. He was nicknamed "Liver Lip" because of his lazy lower lip.

A scene in one *The Lone Ranger* movie required Silver to drag the wounded Lone Ranger to safety as he clung to a saddle stirrup.

"So they brought back Silver number one — good old Liver Lip — for that one scene. He was a real pro and did the drag just perfectly," Moore recalled.

A spectacular rear at Lone Ranger Rock, a cry of "Hi Yo, Silver! Away!!!" and Silver and the Lone Ranger gallop away, ending another episode.

The Lone Ranger debuted on radio in 1933.

Samson

The best friend a prince could have was a handsome white stallion named Samson.

In a fairy tale world of magic wands, dreadful curses, and a fire-breathing dragon, Samson stood hoof-to-toe with his master, Prince Phillip, and was his closest confidant, consulted by the prince on many important matters.

Gifted with intelligence (not speech), Samson communicated with Prince Phillip with nods of his head for "yes;" a sideways headshake for "no;" and whinnies to warn of danger.

On one fateful day, he and Phillip trotted along happily through a forest near a woodcutter's cottage. In the distance they heard a girl singing — a lovely voice she had! — and Phillip halted Samson. Phillip wanted to meet her. But Samson, in a fit of schoolboy jealousy, tried to trot away, unwilling to share Phillip's company. The clever prince, with a promise of extra oats and carrots, convinced Samson to help him search, and a happy nod of Samson's head agreed to the bribe.

The prince and the girl meet, on her sixteenth birthday; they dance, and sing, and fall in love. Neither could know that she was a princess named Aurora or that they, as children, had been promised to each other in marriage.

They also didn't know, as told in Disney's Sleeping Beauty, that the evil Maleficent had cast a spell: Aurora would prick her finger on a spinning wheel spindle and die before sunset on her sixteenth birthday. She was hidden, for her safety, for those sixteen years by three good fairies — Flora, Fauna, and Merryweather. Fortunately, Merryweather was able to weaken the curse, allowing Aurora to fall into a deep, death-like sleep and then be awakened by her true love's kiss.

The sixteen years were almost past. Not knowing that she would go home that evening to her father's castle, she invited Prince Phillip to visit. Arriving at the cottage, he dismounted and turned to look at Samson. With a twinkle in his eye, Samson nodded, as if to say, "Go ahead…good luck!"

Aurora wasn't there, but Maleficent's goons were! They captured Samson and Phillip and chained them up in Maleficent's castle. As the sun set, Maleficent tricked Aurora into pricking her finger, and the princess, fulfilling the wicked prophecy, fell into a deep sleep.

All looked lost until the good fairies showed up. Their magic cut the chains and armed Prince Phillip with a shield of virtue and a sword of truth. He bounded onto Samson and off they galloped to rescue Aurora, leaping yawning canyons, scrambling over a crumbling drawbridge, and battling through a forest of thorns that enveloped Maleficent's castle.

Prince Phillip could always count on Samson.

Time and again, Samson and Phillip overcame the obstacles Maleficent devised to keep the prince from Aurora. Finally, in a thundering rage, she morphed into a fire-breathing dragon. Phillip slashed at her with his enchanted sword, Samson reared and pawed the air, and they dodged her fire and razor-sharp teeth. When Phillip fell from the saddle, Samson stood nearby to see Phillip kill her.

Prince Phillip found Aurora, kissed her, she awoke, and all ended happily as fairy tales should.

The Legend of

Broken-down, one-eyed old Gunpowder clopped along, carrying the gangly schoolteacher Ichabod Crane. Ichabod fretted and fidgeted and glanced about as Gunpowder tramped deeper into the woods.

Ghosts, ghouls, goblins, and one particularly nasty apparition — the Headless Horseman — were said to haunt this little glen called Sleepy Hollow and the peaceable people of Tarry Town, New York.

Poor Ichabod. He was journeying home from a grand party at the estate of Baltus Van Tassel. Music, dancing, and the most delectable foods of all descriptions made the evening delightful indeed. Ichabod reveled in the autumnal bounty, but attend-

Was Daredevil the Headless Horseman's fiery mount?

Sleepy Hollow

ed primarily to woo and win the lovely Katrina, the Van Tassels' only child and heir to their fortune. In attendance, too, was the town prankster Abraham "Brom Bones" Van Brunt, who harbored his own dreams of marrying Katrina.

Brom Bones glared with jealousy as he watched Ichabod and Katrina dance. So he created his own audience, telling of his breathless encounter with the Headless Horseman who rode the black demon horse and menaced passersby in the night.

When the party ended, Katrina (in no uncertain terms) spurned Ichabod's romantic overtures. So now he rode home, rejected and dejected, riding Gunpowder through the haunted woods. Said the storyteller of Ichabod's tale, it was "the very witching time of night…"

A ghost behind that tree, a goblin perched on a low-hanging branch, the Headless Horseman poised to pounce! He kicked Gunpowder harder in the ribs.

The storyteller went on: "In the dark shadow of the grove on the margin of the brook he beheld something huge, misshapen, black, and towering. It stirred not, but seemed gathered up in the gloom, like some gigantic monster ready to spring upon the traveller." Ichabod's heart pounded. Every hair on his head was electrified.

The apparition stepped forward and began to trail Ichabod. Ichabod started singing…then dared a glance. **EEEEK!!!** The rider was headless, the head cradled in the saddle.

With black cape flying, the Headless Horseman charged on his goblin horse. Nostrils flaring, black coat sweating, eyes red with fury.

Ichabod's heels dug into Gunpowder, eking out every ounce of the horse's energy to reach the churchyard bridge. (Legend said the Headless Horseman would vanish in fire and brimstone before crossing it.)

Almost there…and across! Ichabod looked again just as the scepter rose in his stirrups and hurled the head which crashed into Ichabod's head. Ichabod went flying.

Was this Headless Horseman the ghost of a Hessian trooper who searched futilely for his head lost in the Revolutionary War? Or was he that trickster Brom Bones riding his horse Daredevil?

Gunpowder, Ichabod Crane's borrowed, decrepit old horse

The next morning, Gunpowder was found grazing at his owner's gate. Ichabod's hat and a smashed pumpkin lay just beyond the bridge. And villagers never saw Ichabod again.

"The Legend of Sleepy Hollow," first published in 1819, was a short story written by Washington Irving (1783–1859).

The Piebald

Young Velvet Brown, with the passion of Juliet and the conviction of St. Catherine, loved horses:

"Oh, God, give me horses, give me horses! Let me be the best rider in England!"

Just a sprite of a girl, she dreamed big. First her heart was set on winning a horse in a local raffle. When she won the piebald gelding (piebald means a spotted horse), he showed off by jumping everything designed to fence him in.

The dream grew bigger. She decided (with the help of her father's hired hand, Mi Taylor) to train and enter The Pie in the world's greatest race — the Grand National Steeplechase.

Girls, however, were not allowed to ride in the National. Determined not to be denied, she cut her hair, dressed in racing silks, and rode head-to-head against them all. She and The Pie beat the best…and she could claim to be "the best rider in England!"

The 1944 Metro-Goldwyn-Mayer movie, based on the 1935 novel *National Velvet* by Enid Bagnold (Lady Jones), starred a chestnut named King Charles as The Pie, twelve-year-old Elizabeth Taylor as Velvet Brown, and Mickey Rooney as Mi.

The Piebald and Velvet Brown starred in the book and movie *National Velvet*.

His Honour, A Houyhnhnm

As if surviving as a giant in the land of Lilliputians isn't unreasonable enough, English ship Captain Lemuel Gulliver voyaged from England again in 1710, suffered mutiny by his crew, then was abandoned on an island inhabited by thoughtful horses endowed with the gift of speech.

The Houyhnhnms — say it fast, like a horse whinny — star in Part IV of Jonathan Swift's *Gulliver's Travels*. The word houyhnhnm in the horses' language means "horse" and "the perfection of nature."

The Houyhnhnms used their hooves like fingers, conferred every four years in a grand council, boasted refined manners at the manger, and boiled their oats in milk. They were incapable of falsehoods and never "said the thing which was not."

Gulliver learned the horses' language during his five-year stay on the island of Houyhnhnmland from a gray steed whom he called "my master" and "his Honour."

Also inhabiting the island were tree-climbing Yahoos — filthy, hairy, howling, human-like creatures — who labored for the Houyhnhnms and lived in

Captain Gulliver talks with the Houyhnhnms.

kennels and the fields. Gulliver, sadly recognizing they shared their species, abhorred and hated the Yahoos.

Gulliver's "master" was ever curious about Gulliver's physical similarities to the Yahoos: where he came from, why he wore clothes, his ability to reason, his civilities and cleanliness — all so unlike the stinky Yahoos.

Gulliver saw in the gentle Houyhnhnms a cultivated tribe, "naturally disposed to every virtue, wholly governed by reason…"

Misty of Chincoteague

She was a pretty little thing, descended from a wild bunch — free roaming ponies, browsing on salt grass, swimming in ocean surf, huddling as one against winter winds on a barrier island called Assateague Island.

She was born to a mare named Phantom and the stallion Pied Piper, and found fame in Marguerite Henry's 1947 book *Misty of Chincoteague*.

Real children Maureen and Paul Beebe lived with their grandparents on Chincoteague Island, Virginia, a seven-mile long island tucked between Assateague and Virginia and Maryland's Eastern Shores. They admired Phantom, the wild chestnut pony who freely roamed Assateague. They dreamed of owning her and hoped she would be one of the ponies rounded up on Pony Penning Day. They also knew her cunning in escaping the men who herded the ponies across the channel from Assateague to Chincoteague Island. But they worked hard gathering oysters and clams to sell and raise money to buy her at the auction.

For the first time, Paul could go along. He and his pony boarded the boat and rode out to the island. Riding alone, he spied Phantom threading her way through the myrtle bushes and pines. In and out! There! Then gone. He saw something else. A coat of silver and gold that reflected light like mist in the sunshine.

Paul told Maureen, "When I was in the woods there on Assateague, I couldn't tell if I was seeing white mist with the sun on it, or a live colt. The minute I knew 'twas a live colt, I kept calling her Misty in my mind." And so she was named.

Now the children wanted to buy both.

Phantom and Misty were corralled with other ponies and herded to the shoreline. Phantom jumped in, but Misty hesitated. Phantom was cunning like a fox, having twice escaped by circling 'round, away from the herd. This time she circled back to encourage her filly into the water.

Would the Beebe grandchildren have enough money to buy both Misty and Phantom? With wildness and a love of freedom coursing through their veins, could either be content on Chincoteague Island?

(*Misty of Chincoteague* is a work of fiction but is based on real people, real events, and the real pony, Misty. Her memory is cherished today on Chincoteague Island. In 1961, her hoof prints were cast in concrete and author Marguerite Henry autographed "Misty" in the concrete for her. The memorial is displayed today in front of the Island Theatre. In 1997, the Misty of Chincoteague Foundation commissioned her likeness in bronze, which welcomes visitors on Main Street. When Misty died in 1972, her body was preserved for display, as was her daughter Stormy.)

Misty's statue on Chincoteague Island (Virginia) welcomes visitors.

Black Beauty

This timeless tale features a twist. Black Beauty tells his story in first-person narrative (rather, first horse).

Life for Beauty began in "a large pleasant meadow," frolicking with friends, near his mother. There were shade trees for coolness and a shed for warmth. As he grew up, he was sold again and again, ridden until crippled over stony roads, pulling a carriage by hard-handed drivers as well a cab. Beauty also recalls happy homes when he was cherished and considered family.

In chapter twelve, Beauty — drawing on his animal instincts — saves his passengers when he refuses to cross a washed-out bridge. On returning home, his frantic mistress asked if there had been an accident.

Black Beauty

"No, my dear," his master replied. "But if your Black Beauty had not been wiser than we were, we should have been carried down the river at the wooden bridge."

Beauty remembered: "Oh, what a good supper he gave me that night — a good bran mash and some crushed beans with my oats — and such a thick, comfortable bed of straw!

"And I was glad of it, for I was tired."

Black Beauty was written by British novelist Anna Sewell. She was crippled and relied on horses and carriages to get around. From her home in Old Catton, she watched horse-drawn carriages pass. Horses' heads held high and tight by bearing reins; overworked horses beaten until bloody; horses limping and lame, whipped to move on; she saw it all and grieved. She wrote *Black Beauty* to protest cruel treatment of horses.

Black Beauty was Anna Sewell's only book. She was paid £20 for the manuscript and died a few months after its publication in 1877.

Merrylegs

Merrylegs, a chubby gray pony in the novel *Black Beauty*, lived in the stall next to Beauty's at Squire Gordon's farm.

Merrylegs and Beauty were friends and enjoyed a fine home and good care. The little pony was a trusted member of the squire's family.

"Why, I am as careful of our young ladies as the master could be, and as for the little ones, it is I who teach them to ride. I am the best friend and the best riding master those children have," Merrylegs told Beauty.

Troubled one day with some boys who rode him too long and too hard and whipped him with a stick, he taught them a lesson. "Boys, you see, think a horse or pony can go on as long and as fast as they please. They never think that a pony can get tired or have any feelings." He reared and let them slide off his back.

"…I can tell you good places make good horses," he said to the abused horse Ginger.

Merrylegs

Mr. Butler

Bonnie Blue Butler aimed her handsome pony Mr. Butler at the jump, which, at Bonnie's insistence, had been raised to a foot and a half.

Outfitted like the four-year-old southern belle she was, she rode Mr. Butler sidesaddle in a blue velvet riding habit and matching hat, topped with a red plume. (The plume honored the plumed Civil War hero Major General J.E.B. Stuart.)

Bonnie's father, Rhett, was concerned the jump was too high.

"When you are six years old," said Rhett. "Then you'll be big enough for a higher jump and I'll buy you a bigger horse. Mr. Butler's legs aren't long enough."

Bonnie argued: "They are, too. I jumped Aunt Melly's rose bushes and they are 'normously high!'"

"No, you must wait," insisted Rhett. But he lost the battle of wills to Bonnie.

Rhett and her mother, Scarlett O'Hara Butler, watched Bonnie ride Mr. Butler to the jump, their eyes trained on every move of pony and child. Then, a memory rushed at Scarlett, the details as vivid as if it happened only yesterday. A dreadful memory. She had watched her father riding one day and take a jump. He fell off and died instantly.

As if on cue, Bonnie, too, fell off Mr. Butler and died in front of her parents, a tragedy from which Rhett never recovered.

Mr. Butler, Bonnie Blue, Scarlett, and Rhett were characters in Margaret Mitchell's beloved Civil War-era novel *Gone with the Wind*.

Mr. Butler and Bonnie Blue Butler

The Black Stallion

On a night dark as pitch, Alec Ramsay is hurled from his bed aboard the steamer Drake. The ship is sinking off the coast of Portugal. People are screaming, fighting for places in the lifeboats. Alec stumbles among the chaos. Then he remembers the proud black stallion, trapped in a stall, a horse he'd befriended over the past few weeks.

Alec fights his way to the "Black," opens his door, and the wild desert horse jumps overboard, a rope trailing his massive body. As he leaps, the horse grazes Alec and Alec is pitched into the sea behind him.

Fighting for breath and life, Alec rises to the surface as the Drake sinks. No lifeboats, no help. Just then, the Black swims close and Alec grabs the rope.

As if returning the favor for saving him, the Black swims all night and pulls Alec to a deserted island. There, they save each other, surviving on scant food and their friendship. Then Alec sees a freighter offshore.

"Alec flung his arms around the Black's neck and buried his head in the long mane. 'We're leaving together, Black — together,' he said." The ship's captain will take Alec, but not the horse.

"He saved my life, Captain. I can't leave him here alone. He'll die!" The Black comes onboard and, as Alec promised, they are rescued together. Alec and former jockey Henry Dailey train the Black — "the mystery horse" — for the racetrack.

Walter Farley's *The Black Stallion*, a classic in children's literature, is a boy-and-his-horse adventure. Published in 1941, the book spurred sequels (written by Farley and later by his son Steven), an award-winning movie, and television series.

Alec Ramsay tamed the Black Stallion.

Mister Ed

If Black Beauty can talk to his friends, why can't Mister Ed talk to Wilbur?

And so he did on television for six seasons and 143 episodes. But only to Wilbur!

Mister Ed lived in Wilbur and Carol Post's backyard barn. He talked on the phone, played baseball with the Los Angeles Dodgers, surfed, sang, and flirted with fillies.

Former parade horse Bamboo Harvester played Mister Ed. His co-star, Alan Young, praised the handsome Palomino: "Ed handled his part with superb professionalism…How can you tire of discussing the handsomest and greatest actor you ever worked with? An actor who was humble, always ready to please, asked for so little, and carried me on his back all the way."

The series debuted January 5, 1961, and ran in syndication until July 2, 1961. CBS ran *Mister Ed* from October 1, 1961, to February 6, 1966. In 1997, *TV Guide* named Mister Ed's Dodger game episode — "Leo Durocher Meets Mister Ed" — No. 73 in its "100 Greatest Episodes of all Time" recap.

Mister Ed still entertains on television and DVDs.

Mister Ed talked *only* to Wilbur.

Flicka

Ken McLaughlin wanted one thing in this world. His own horse. One forever his.

On a working ranch, good horses are sold for good money. He was thrilled when his dad granted his wish and told him to choose his horse from the newborn foals running with their mothers on the range.

Early one morning, as the world was waking, Ken rode out to pasture. Then he saw her, the sorrel daughter of a mare named Rocket. She ran past him in a moment of fear, and they exchanged glances.

Flicka and Ken McLaughlin (played by Roddy McDowell) from the television series

In that split second, Ken knew she would belong to him.

"He hadn't had to choose one after all. She had just come to him. His own because of that second's cry for help that had come from her eyes to his; his own because of her wild beauty and speed, his own because his heart burned within him at the sight and thought of her; his own because – well, just his own."

Ken's father she said was crazy; that she came from crazy stock; that she was "loco." But Ken loved her and named her Flicka, which in Swedish means "little girl."

Caught and confined, Flicka grieved for her freedom and nearly killed herself on a barbed-wire fence she tried to jump, her delicate skin torn and tattered, in a desperate attempt to reach the open range she knew. Ken nursed her; she remained indifferent. When he carried a can of oats to her, she nickered. Maybe it was the oats that thrilled her...but Ken fell in love all over again.

Then Ken saved her life while almost losing his own. And she was his.

My Friend Flicka, published in 1941, was written by Mary O'Hara (real name: Mary O'Hara Alsop), on a Wyoming ranch near Cheyenne. Her story of Flicka inspired a television series and several movies.

Champion

A stable of champions helped Gene Autry become the cowboy-singing superstar that he was.

Gene was a songwriter (who hasn't heard "Here Comes Santa Claus," a song he co-wrote?), an astute businessman, and movie/television/radio star. His equine sidekicks, all named Champion, starred alongside him in movies, on television, and in personal appearances. There were three "official" Champions, while other Champions made contributions unique to their special skills.

The first Champion earned his first on-screen credit in 1935's *Melody Trail*. He was a striking sorrel with a long, wide white blaze down his face. You can recognize him by his three white stockings and single dark right front leg. He died at seventeen in 1943.

The second Champion (Champion Jr., also a sorrel) starred with Gene in movies until 1950 and was billed as "Wonder Horse of the West." He traveled by boat for special appearances in England and Cuba. The third Champion was Television Champion and Gene's favorite, a flashy part-Arabian with a flaxen mane and tail who co-starred in Gene's last movies, in TV's *The Gene Autry Show* (1950–1955) and *The Adventures of Champion* (1955–1956). This Champion died of old age at twenty-five.

Other Champions made their own histories: Lindy Champion (born on May 20, 1927, the day Charles Lindbergh took off to fly solo from New York to Paris) was the first horse to fly transcontinental from California to New York, where he appeared in 1940 in New York City's venerable Madison Square Garden. Touring Champion took high tea in 1953 at the swank Savoy Hotel in London.

Gene's Champions could play dead, dance, do the hula, pray, come to his whistle, jump through rings of fire, and answer questions with a "yes" or "no" head nod. And always make their master look like the hero.

Gene's boot prints and handprints and Touring Champion's hoofprints were cast in the forecourt of Hollywood's Grauman's Chinese Theatre on December 23, 1949.

Champion and Gene Autry starred in the *Melody Trail*.

The Maltese Cat

The Maltese Cat led his Skidars team to victory against the well-heeled Archangels.

"A flea-bitten horse never tires."

ENGLISH PROVERB

The Maltese Cat was not a cat at all. He was a flea-bitten gray horse and hero of the Rudyard Kipling same-titled short story.

"The Maltese Cat" is a polo pony and tells about a polo match in India between his team, the Skidars (from a poor British infantry regiment), and well-bred horses from the wealthy Archangels team.

"The Maltese Cat knew that bamboos grew solely in order that poloballs might be turned from their roots, that grain was given to ponies to keep them in hard condition, and that ponies were shod to prevent them slipping on a turn."

The Maltese Cat's clever and inspired direction of his teammates shows that he is the real team captain, not his rider, Lutyens. Kipling presents the underlying theme that wealth and patrician breeding are equalized on the playing field.

"The Maltese Cat" is considered one of the English language's finest descriptions of a game. Dolly Bobs, Kipling's own gray horse, inspired the Maltese Cat character.

3 WAR HORSES

These horses endured the tragedies and enjoyed the triumphs of war with equal grace.

Joey

Joey tells his tale in his own words — a commentary on war, of friends lost and found, of devotion to duty and to those who loved him, and the devotion of others to him.

Young and innocent, a brilliant red-bay stallion eternally willing, British-born Joey is wrenched from his mother and best friend Albert and thrust into the madness of World War I. He succeeds and suffers and somehow makes friends on his journeys to the front, including an especially good friend — Topthorn — a one-horse support system.

Joey reflected as he and Topthorn returned to the battlefront from a respite away:

"We were back among the fearful noise and stench of battle, hauling our gun through the mud, urged on and sometimes whipped on by men who displayed little care or interest in our welfare just so long as we got the guns where they had to go. It was not that they were cruel men, but just that they seemed to be driven now by a fearful compulsion that left no room and no time for pleasantness or consideration either for each other or for us."

Author Michael Morpurgo was inspired to write *War Horse* by an oil painting that hangs in the former school in his village. Under the painting are the words: "Joey. Painted by Captain James Nicholls, Autumn 1914."

Though his words were created by the author, Joey's experiences reflect the heartache and hardship experienced by two enemies fighting each other. Everyone seemed to come out better having known Joey. But…will Albert ever come back into his life?

In London on Park Lane stands the Animals In War Memorial, a reminder of the sacrifices made by millions of horses, mules, dogs, and sundry animals in wars past and present. HRH The Princess Royal, Princess Anne, unveiled the statue in 2004.

Joey in *War Horse*

Midnight Ride of Paul Revere

Paul Revere's Horse

"I set off upon a very good Horse; it was then about 11 o'Clock, and very pleasant."

PAUL REVERE

On a moonlit night in colonial Boston, Paul Revere sat silently as friends rowed him across the Charles River, waves lapping against the boat's wooden hull, past a moored British warship. Revere stepped onto the opposite shore.

(Continued on next page)

Paul Revere's Horse (continued)

A Sons of Liberty member and spy for the cause of colonial independence from Great Britain, Revere was on mission. A new country's future hung in the balance. He needed a horse that night of April 18, 1775, with qualities he boasted himself — smart, steadfast, and ready to ride in a minute.

He made his way to Charlestown and Samuel Larkin's barn, where Samuel's son, church deacon John Larkin, loaned him a horse.

Revere must ride to Lexington and warn patriot leaders Samuel Adams and John Hancock that British troops — called "regulars" — had crossed the Charles River and were coming to arrest them. The British would then march on to Concord to capture rebel supplies.

Before leaving Boston, Revere asked a friend to hang two lanterns in the Old North Church steeple, signaling that British soldiers had crossed the Charles River.

The Larkin horse was readied and Revere stepped into the stirrup. "I got a Horse of Deacon Larkin." They took off as the "Moon shone bright."

Revere soon encountered British mounted officers. "I turned my horse short, about, and rid upon a full Gallop for Mistick Road, he followed me about 300 Yardes, and finding He could not catch me, returned…"

Revere spurred his horse on, waking the countryside, calling patriots to arms. Shutters flew wide, doors creaked open, sleeping households jerked awake.

"In Medford, I awaked the Captain of the Minute men; and after that, I alarmed almost every House, till I got to Lexington."

Revere delivered his message to Adams and Hancock — "The regulars are coming out." He then set out for Concord, joined by courier William Dawes and Dr. Samuel Prescott, another Sons of Liberty.

Suddenly, into the moonlight stepped horses ridden by British soldiers, and the three couriers split up. Dr. Prescott jumped his horse over a low stone wall and escaped. Revere, attempting his getaway, was caught by six British officers who ordered him to dismount, then questioned him.

Dawes got away, too, galloping his horse wildly, "slapping his leather breeches" as armed soldiers followed in hot pursuit. Dawes pulled up at a nearby farmhouse ("thrown to the ground by the suddenness with which he had been forced to check his horse"), stood up and shouted: "Halloo, my boys! I've got two of 'em."

Thinking they were in the crosshairs of an ambush, the British soldiers turned tail and galloped away. In fact, the farmhouse was empty and Dawes disappeared into the night. Only Dr. Prescott reached Concord.

And so Revere faced the British soldiers alone as a traitor, guilty of treason, a crime punishable by death.

Major Edward Mitchell ordered Revere to answer his questions truthfully. Brave and forthright, Revere told Major Mitchell that he was, indeed, a courier for the cause of independence and his name was Revere. He mounted up again, joined by four other arrested patriots, and they all rode toward Lexington.

In the early-morning quiet, gunfire was heard coming from Lexington Green. Major Mitchell gave Revere's horse to his sergeant, whose horse was tired. Now afoot, Revere walked to Lexington and arrived not long before British soldiers shot and killed eight colonial "minutemen," igniting the American Revolution.

What happened to Paul Revere's horse? No one knows. No one even knows the horse's name. Though never confirmed, Larkin family tradition claims the horse of Revere's famous midnight ride was the family's mare Brown Beauty.

Traveller

Traveller expected a day filled with whinnies of horses and screams of men and the pop! pop! pop! of gunfire. He expected more sounds of war to come his way this day —

(Continued on next page)

Traveller and Robert E. Lee enjoy a ride near Lexington, Virginia, 1866.

Traveller (continued)

April 9, 1865.

But as the morning fog burned away, quiet settled over central Virginia. And Traveller saw something new, a white flag carried on horseback. This day brought Palm Sunday and the beginning of the end of the terrible Civil War.

Traveller and General Robert E. Lee were soldiers, fighting for the Confederate States of America — the South. The South wanted a new country. So brother fought brother for four bloody years. Traveller carried General Lee into the war's biggest battles, including Antietam, the Wilderness, Gettysburg, and this last one — Appomattox.

On April 9, Traveller carried his master on a mission of peace.

Over the past two days, 800 soldiers from both sides had been killed or hurt. General Lee's soldiers could fight no more. He mounted Traveller and rode west toward the village of Appomattox Court House to meet with Lieutenant General Ulysses S. Grant, general-in-chief of the United States Armies. They would discuss terms under which the Confederate States Army of Northern Virginia would surrender.

General Lee wore his best uniform, a saber dangled at his side. Traveller waited outside, as he had so many times before, grazing under the watch of Confederate Private Joshua O. Johns.

Terms were signed and General Lee and Traveller returned to camp. Lieutenant General James Longstreet remembered: "As he passed they raised their heads and looked upon him with swimming eyes. Those who could find voice said goodby, those who could not speak and were near, passed their hands gently over the sides of Traveller."

Another soldier recalled that Traveller "always acknowledged the cheers of the troops by tosses of his head and the men frequently cheered him for it, to which he would answer back as often as they did." And on April 9, "his head was tossing a return to the salutes all along the line."

On April 12, Traveller carried General Lee in the rain toward home in Richmond. A minister saw them pass. "(Traveller) was bespattered with mud, and his head hung down as if worn by long traveling."

Good food, peaceful rest, and each other's quiet company helped Traveller and Lee recover from the war's terrors. And happy years followed.

General Lee became president of Washington College in Lexington, Virginia, and Traveller (the general called his color "confederate grey") moved into a cozy brick stable. The two former warriors enjoyed daily rides, but the war had scarred Traveller.

"Have patience with Traveller," Lee implored a blacksmith trimming Traveller's hooves. "He was made nervous by the bursting of bombs around him during the war."

Traveller is interred near Lee Chapel at the college now called Washington and Lee University.

"How is Traveller? Tell him I miss him dreadfully and have repented of our separation but once and that is the whole time since we parted."
— General Lee, in a letter home

Cincinnati

Contrasting Traveller and Robert E. Lee were Cincinnati and Ulysses S. Grant.

While Traveller and Lee wore gray hair and uniforms of the Southern Confederacy, Cincinnati and Grant wore the North's dark blue and dark hair. The four met time and time again during the Civil War and finally, in a prelude to peace, in the Virginia village of Appomattox Court House.

After the Union defeated Southern forces at the Siege of Vicksburg (ending July 4, 1863), Major General Grant was summoned to visit a dying man named S. S. Grant (no relation) at the Lindell Hotel in St. Louis. His wish: to provide the general with "the finest horse in the world" for the war. Grant received the horse — a dark bay, 17-hand son of the great Thoroughbred racehorse Lexington — with the stipulation that he be well treated. Grant named his new war charger Cincinnati.

Cincinnati carried Grant on major engagements until the war's end, including Cold Harbor and Appomattox. Few rode Cincinnati; exceptions were President Abraham Lincoln and Admiral Daniel Ammen, a boyhood friend.

"Lincoln spent the latter days of his life with me. (During) the last month of the war (he) was with me all the time. He was a fine horseman and rode my horse 'Cincinnati' every day," Grant wrote. Grant once refused $10,000 for Cincinnati.

Cincinnati survived the war and died in 1878 of old age on Admiral Ammen's Maryland farm.

Confederate Lieutenant General James Longstreet, a classmate of Grant's at the United States Military Academy at West Point, praised Grant: "In horsemanship...he was noted as the most proficient in the Academy. In fact, rider and horse held together like the fabled centaur..."

Cincinnati and Major General Ulysses S. Grant at the Battle of Cold Harbor, Virginia, June 1864

Little Sorrel

May 2, 1863
American Civil War
Chancellorsville Campaign
Spotsylvania, Virginia

"Stonewall" Jackson rode Little Sorrel forward into the moonlight to scout attack positions and plan strategy for another day in the Battle of Chancellorsville.

Lieutenant General Thomas J. "Stonewall" Jackson, serving the Confederate States of America under General Robert E. Lee, was optimistic. The Army of Northern Virginia had outsmarted Union Major General Joseph Hooker, and the outnumbered Confederates had outflanked the "bluecoats." Victory was in the offing.

Safe in Little Sorrel's saddle, accompanied by staff, Jackson completed his reconnaissance and about-faced to return to his Confederate battle lines. Then, from the darkened trees, a shot! Several shots! The shooters targeted the shadowy silhouettes riding toward them. Jackson grabbed his left shoulder as blood oozed through his gray uniform, shot three times by soldiers of the 18th North Carolina regiment. His own men had mistaken his party for Union cavalry.

Little Sorrel bolted and ran down Old Mountain Road as Jackson tottered in his saddle. Captain Richard E. Wilbourn grabbed Little Sorrel's bridle and helped Jackson dismount, then he and General A. P. Hill cut open Jackson's jacket and shirt to stop the bleeding.

At first, Jackson's wounds did not seem life-threatening. But his left arm was so badly damaged it was amputated. Bad went to worse when Jackson contracted pneumonia and his condition deteriorated. The Battle of Chancellorsville, known as "Lee's greatest victory," raged until May 6 and ended in a Confederate victory. But Lee had lost Jackson, his second-in-command, who died on May 10.

❧

Like all horses and mules, Little Sorrel knew nothing of North and South conflicts. He might have wondered why he was loaded with other horses into a railroad car as he bounced and balanced his weight as the train chugged along.

The train, bound for Washington and northern commands, was intercepted by Confederate soldiers in Harpers Ferry, West Virginia. Jackson, thinking him a nice size and temperament, bought him for his wife. After finding his gait "as easy as the rocking of a cradle,"

Jackson decided to keep him to ride in the war.

Unlike his master, Little Sorrel was immune to fatal injury. He survived the Battle of Manassas (1861), the Valley Campaign of 1862, the Seven Days Battles (June, July 1862), the Battle of Fredericksburg (December 1862), and finally, Chancellorsville.

Jackson's widow, Mary Anna, honored Little Sorrel as a war hero, and she and her family enjoyed his company when he was sent to North Carolina. So clever was he during retirement that he learned to unlock his stable door, then unlock the doors of his stable mates to lead all out to graze.

Little Sorrel "seemed absolutely indefatigable," Mary Anna wrote. "His eyes were his chief beauty, being most intelligent and expressive, and as soft as a gazelle's. He had a peculiar habit of lying down like a dog when the command halted for rest."

Little Sorrel later moved to Virginia Military Institute in Lexington, Virginia (where Jackson once taught) and then to the Soldiers' Home in Richmond, where he died at a very elderly age of thirty-six. His hide is on display at VMI, and his remains are interred on the parade grounds near Jackson's statue.

Stonewall Jackson on Little Sorrel

Winchester

Winchester was a Civil War marathoner. The big black Morgan ran as if the world depended on him. For the Army of the Shenandoah, it did.

On October 18, 1864, he and Union Major General Philip Sheridan were overnighting in Winchester, Virginia. The next morning, Sheridan heard cannons firing in the Shenandoah Valley. He saddled his horse (called Rienzi then, pronounced *rye in zee*) and rode south toward Middletown. He soon encountered retreating Union troops, many dazed and panicked.

Sheridan rode faster. Rienzi delivered Sheridan a wild ride "12 miles distant" and into the fray. Confederate Lieutenant General Jubal Early had launched surprise attacks on the Army of the Shenandoah — Sheridan's soldiers in blue — and the Confederacy held the valley.

With the strategic Shenandoah Valley at stake, Sheridan mobilized quickly, galloping Rienzi among the men, waving his hat and shouting encouragement, rallying the army to counterattack. By nightfall, the Federals had beaten the Confederates back across Cedar Creek and down the valley. All hopes of the Confederacy holding the Shenandoah Valley evaporated.

Rienzi, a descendant of the swift Morgan stallion Black Hawk, was purchased in 1862 for Sheridan when the 2nd Michigan Cavalry was encamped in Rienzi, Mississippi. After the Battle of Cedar Creek, Sherman called him Winchester. They fought in more than forty engagements and were present at Appomattox Court House when the Army of Northern Virginia signed surrender papers to the Army of the Potomac.

Sheridan praised Winchester as "an animal of great intelligence and immense strength and endurance."

Thomas Buchanan Read's poem "Sheridan's Ride" honors Winchester. (Remember "Paul Revere's Ride" — another famous poem from another war that made another horse and rider famous?)

Winchester enjoyed a peaceful retirement and died in 1878. His body was preserved and is displayed in the Smithsonian Institution's National Museum of American History in Washington, D.C.

Winchester on display in the National Museum of American History, Smithsonian Institution, Washington, D.C.

Black Jack

The four-beat cadence of the riderless horse echoed the beat of a country's broken heart.

On November 22, 1963, President John F. Kennedy was assassinated in Dallas, Texas. The world watched in shock as a two-day state funeral followed in Washington, D.C.: the president's body lying in state; religious rites in St. Matthew's Cathedral; American flags flying at half-staff; the grave at Arlington National Cemetery. And Black Jack.

(Continued on next page)

Black Jack (continued)

Black Jack paraded in a place of privilege in the processions, only a few feet behind the 1918 artillery caisson that bore the President's coffin draped in an American flag. His empty saddle symbolized an ancient military tradition of mourning the leader who will ride no more. In the saddle's stirrups was a pair of spit-shined black boots, reversed and facing backward, allowing the leader to review his troops one last time. A silver saber hung on Black Jack's right side.

As President of the United States, Kennedy was commander-in-chief. Black Jack was on a mission from the Caisson Platoon, part of the U.S. Army's Third U.S. Infantry — "The Old Guard" — based at Fort Myer, Virginia.

Black Jack was a Morgan-Quarter Horse from Oklahoma. His normal duty was escorting American heroes to gravesites in peaceful Arlington National Cemetery. President Kennedy's funeral was in downtown Washington. There were drums, bagpipes, crowds lining the streets.

Handling Black Jack was nineteen-year-old Pfc. Arthur Carlson, a six-foot, two-inch tall army soldier from Alabama. He had his hands full.

Carlson said Black Jack was hardest to control "when I was supposed to be standing still, like outside the White House, outside the Capitol, and outside the cathedral, where he stomped my foot.

"At the time, I was in full military mode; that is, completely focused on the mission. That was it. I didn't allow anything else in. I was just trying to do my small part the best I could."

Carlson's and Black Jack's "small part" remains an enduring image of the Kennedy funeral.

Black Jack, the riderless horse, during President Kennedy's funeral in Washington, D.C., 1963

Old Bob

Old Bob served President Abraham Lincoln just as Black Jack served President John F. Kennedy, almost 100 years later.

President Lincoln had owned Old Bob, but gave him to a friend in Springfield, Illinois, when he moved to Washington, D.C., to become president of the United States.

When President Lincoln was shot in Washington on April 14, 1865, and died the next morning, he was mourned at a funeral in the nation's capital, just as Kennedy would be. Lincoln's body then traveled by train to Springfield for burial.

In Springfield on May 4, sixteen-year-old Old Bob walked behind the funeral hearse, wearing a silver-trimmed mourning blanket and led by the Reverend Henry Brown, who had worked for the Lincolns. Six black horses, their headstalls carrying huge black plumes, pulled the $6,000 hearse borrowed from the city of St. Louis.

"A splendid old horse of dark bay color with swelling nostrils and eyes of an eagle," praised an admirer.

Old Bob's role in President Lincoln's funeral made the dark bay, sway-backed horse something of a celebrity. Reverend Brown did his best to ward off souvenir hunters snatching at his tail hairs. Old Bob also starred in the Union's victory parade after the surrender of General Robert E. Lee's Confederate States Army of Northern Virginia on April 9.

Old Bob paraded in a place of honor during the funeral procession of assassinated President Abraham Lincoln, Springfield, Illinois, 1865. Attending Old Bob were an unidentified man, left, and his then-owner John Flynn.

Bucephalus

The mighty Bucephalus was matched in strength and daring only by his master, Alexander the Great.

The fourteen-year-old black stallion was presented to the court of Alexander's father, King Philip II of Macedonia. The beautiful and powerful horse pawed and kicked and reared, unwilling to be approached, certainly not ridden. Philip ordered him taken away.

Twelve-year-old Alexander was watching and stepped forward to tell his father: "What an excellent horse do they lose for want of address and boldness to manage him!" He promised to pay for him if he couldn't tame him.

Alexander saw that the stallion was frightened of his shadow. So he turned him toward the sun, spoke softly, gentled him, and rode him away. From that moment, the stallion was his forever.

King Philip proudly advised: "O my son, look thee out a kingdom equal to and worthy of thyself, for Macedonia is too little for thee."

Alexander named his horse Bucephalus because his head was broad, like a bull. In 334 B.C., Alexander set out on Bucephalus to conquer the Persian Empire. Within a decade, Alexander had conquered lands about the size of the United States and had changed the world forever by introducing Greek culture.

Legend says that in 327 B.C., when Alexander battled with the Indian King Porus, Bucephalus was speared and, though bleeding to death, carried Alexander to safety before collapsing and dying. Bucephalus lived to be thirty; Alexander died at age thirty-two.

Alexander honored his stallion by naming an Eastern city Bucephalia.

Alexander and Bucephalus

Sergeant Reckless

Looks can be deceiving. A dainty mare with the delicate name of Morning Flame lived a racehorse's life in Korea. Then the Korean War broke out. And in October 1952, U.S. Marine Lieutenant Eric Pederson bought her for $250 and drafted her into the Recoilless "Reckless" Rifle Platoon, Anti-Tank Company, 1st Battalion, 5th Marine Regiment.

Morning Flame ate, slept, and traveled like the Marines. Uncooked oatmeal and bread were her first Marine meal. She loved scrambled eggs, soft drinks, and Hershey chocolate. She learned to lie down and "take cover while on the front lines" and ride in an open-topped 36" x 72" Jeep trailer. She often slept in heated tents with her Marine friends on cold nights.

She fought like a Marine, too, hoof to boot on the battlefield. In the battle Outpost Vegas in 1953, on one day she made fifty-one trips to the front, hauling nearly 9,000 pounds of 75mm recoilless ammunition more than thirty-five miles over hilly terrain, dodging bullets all the way. She sometimes did this duty alone, not led by a Marine...for she knew the way to the front.

Nicknamed Reckless, on April 10, 1954, she earned a battlefield promotion to sergeant and wore silver stripes on her blanket.

On October 17, 1954, during a football game in Korea between the

Sergeant Reckless and her friends from the Recoilless "Reckless" Rifle Platoon. (Below) Sergeant Reckless hauls ammunition to the front during the Korean War.

7th Army Division and the 1st Marine Division, came announcement of her transfer to Camp Pendleton, California, and commendation: "It was in the battle for the outpost Vegas that Reckless proved her merit as a Marine. With enemy artillery and mortar rounds coming in at the rate of 500 a minute, she carried 75mm shells into the front lines. Each yard as a passage under fire...Disregard for her own safety and conduct under fire were an inspiration to the troops and

in keeping with the highest traditions of the Naval Service."

Soon she was traveling to America aboard a freighter and disembarked the ship a celebrity. At Camp Pendleton, she was promoted to staff sergeant and enjoyed rest, peace, food aplenty, and lots of attention. She gave birth to three foals.

Having been wounded twice in Korea, she was awarded two Purple Hearts; the Korean Service Medal with three battle stars; a Presidential Unit Citation with star; the United Nations Service Medal; and the National Defense Service Medal. In 2016, she was awarded the Dickin Medal, England's Victoria Cross for animals.

Sergeant Reckless died in 1968 and a memorial honors her at the Camp Pendleton stables.

Comanche

Comanche cantered innocently into the crosshairs of an American military disaster.

It was a hot Sunday — June 25, 1876. The U.S. Army had sent the Seventh Cavalry to Montana Territory to subdue the Sioux Indians. Expansionism into the American West had intruded on Sioux ancestral homelands. The Sioux, of course, fought back.

(Continued on next page)

Comanche and farrier Samuel J. Winchester at Fort Riley, Kansas, 1891

Comanche (continued)

Lieutenant Colonel George Armstrong Custer entered the Little Bighorn Valley from the south with five companies of soldiers. Comanche and Captain Myles W. Keogh led Company I.

About 2,000 Lakota Sioux, Cheyenne, and Arapahoe warriors lay in wait, anxious for the siege that would become famous as the Battle of the Little Bighorn, Custer's Last Stand, and Battle of the Greasy Grass.

Custer was outnumbered by almost ten to one. Rifle shots cracked, lances flew, arrows found their targets. War cries, screams, mayhem…it was over in less than two hours.

Strewn dead on Last Stand Hill and about the valley were 210 soldiers and officers of the Seventh Cavalry and about seventy cavalry horses. (Fifty-three soldiers from Major Marcus A. Reno's and Captain Frederick W. Benteen's commands were killed several miles away. Fewer than 100 Native Americans died.)

Some warriors remembered a black-mustached man, probably Keogh, taking command after Custer was killed, galloping his war horse among the panicked soldiers, shouting orders. But every soldier in the Custer fight died, and Comanche, wounded seven times, was left for dead.

An army burial party found Comanche two days later "too weak to stand," wrote Theodore W. Goldin. Men scooped up river water in hats for "the poor famished horse." By boat, by wagon, by sheer human will, Comanche arrived at Fort Lincoln to recover.

Regiment commander Colonel Samuel D. Sturgis lost a son at Bighorn and in April 1878 ordered: "(Comanche's) comfort should be a special pride and solicitude on the part of the Seventh Cavalry… Wounded and scarred as he is, his very silence speaks more eloquently than words, of the desperate struggle against over-whelming numbers…"

Goldin later recalled that when the army band played or bugles sounded, "I have seen the old fellow trot to his old place in front of the line of his master's troop."

Comanche lived out his long life at Fort Riley and roamed at will — a pet, a mascot, a revered veteran. He died in 1891 and was mounted for visitors to see at the University of Kansas Natural History Museum, bearing battle scars and cavalry gear.

Vic

Vic and Comanche would have known each other. As favored mounts of Seventh Cavalry officers, together they faced cold and heat, fear and fatigue, and overwhelming odds in the Battle of the Little Bighorn on June 25, 1876.

We know what happened to Comanche. But what about Vic?

Vic — short for Victory — was born in 1864 at Ashland, the elegant Kentucky farm owned by statesman Henry Clay. A fast and flashy Thoroughbred, he was the son of the mare Magnolia and the stallion Uncle Vic, and grandson of the important Thoroughbred Lexington. Reddish in color, boasting a white blaze and four white stockings, he won and finished in the money in numerous Kentucky races.

George Armstrong Custer loved Thoroughbreds and bought Vic, probably in early 1872. Vic's speed helped Lieutenant Colonel Custer hunt game to feed hungry soldiers and outrun Plains Indians who wanted Custer's scalp.

But army life was hard on finely bred Vic. He suffered in Dakota Territory's frigid winters and winds. Custer was known to bring his shivering Vic into his tent and cover him with a blanket.

Custer died with everyone in his five companies, plus attached personnel, scouts, and seventy cavalry horses. Some warriors in the Custer fight recalled seeing Vic in their village; others said he was taken to Canada. Custer's widow, Libbie, insisted Vic died alongside her husband. The fate of the fine Kentucky Thoroughbred remains unknown.

Custer, Vic, and Dogs. Scott Myers, 1980. John M. Carroll collection

Marengo

When Napoleon met his Waterloo, Marengo switched sides and lived out his long life in luxury.

Marengo, light-gray in color, was Napoleon Bonaparte's favorite war charger. A French politician and military genius, Napoleon rose to power soon after the French Revolution and crowned himself emperor. In 1798, Napoleon's forces fought in Egypt; here he found and kept for himself this finely bred stallion.

Marengo stood only about fourteen hands — and Napoleon (contrary to rumors that he was quite short) stood five feet, six inches, and looked taller on diminutive Marengo. When horses were primary instruments of war, military leaders often rode light-colored horses so they could be seen on the battlefield. Marengo fit the bill as Napoleon noted:

"A horse has memory, knowledge, and love…I had a horse myself, who knew me from any other person, and manifested by capering and proudly marching with his head erect, when I was on his back, his knowledge that he bore a person superior to the others by whom he was surrounded."

Marengo was named when Napoleon, not yet emperor of France, rode him in the Battle of Marengo on June 14, 1800, in today's Italy. It was a great Napoleon victory, another step taken in his conquest of Europe. Victory after victory followed, with Marengo in the middle of most of them. On December 2, 1804, Napoleon was crowned emperor of France.

In 1812, Marengo — then nearing twenty years old — carried Napoleon into Russia and back. That campaign was a disaster, Napoleon abdicated, and he was exiled to the French island of Elba.

In less than a year, Napoleon escaped and reseized his throne. But his reign and ownership of Marengo ended on June 18, 1815, on a battlefield near the Belgium village of Waterloo. A coalition of soldiers, including the Anglo-Allied Army led by British commander The Duke of Wellington, crushed Napoleon's troops. Napoleon was exiled again, this time for life, on the British island St. Helena off the African coast.

Marengo fared much better. At Waterloo, the British took him as war booty and he lived the last of his thirty-eight years as a country gentleman.

Marengo's skeleton is displayed at the National Army Museum in London. (The phrase that someone met his or her Waterloo means a catastrophic end for a person or cause.)

The Battle of Marengo

Copenhagen

Copenhagen and The Duke of Wellington, front and center, led the charge against Napoleon Bonaparte in the Battle of Waterloo.

Copenhagen's fractious temperament rivaled the steady and steely nerves of his British owner "The Iron Duke," aka the Duke of Wellington, born Arthur Wellesley.

Napoleon had escaped from exile and marshaled his armies for yet another European conquest. The duke gathered his own allied forces to fight Napoleon on a battlefield in Waterloo, Belgium.

The fighting was fierce, starting at about noon on Sunday, June 18, 1815. It was a draw until Prussian troops arrived to buttress the duke's forces; it ended at about 11 p.m. with England the victor and Napoleon captured.

Soldiers from both sides were bloodied and spent. The weary duke rode Copenhagen to an inn, dismounted, and gave his stallion a good-natured pat on the rump for a job well done. But cranky Copenhagen launched a ferocious kick at his master, which fortunately missed its mark.

Copenhagen was foaled in 1808, a chestnut son of the Thoroughbred stallion Eclipse. His dam, Lady Catherine, was ridden to Denmark during the Napoleonic Wars. She was found to be pregnant and sent home. Her foal was named for the British victory at the Second Battle of Copenhagen in 1801.

As it was with many important military horses ridden by important leaders, Copenhagen survived military service. Unlike many of those horses, he was not white or gray. He retired in England on the duke's seven thousand-acre Stratfield Saye estate, given him by the British government in gratitude for dispatching Napoleon. The Duchess of Wellington and her daughter-in-law treated Copenhagen to chocolate, and he gave them hair for bracelets.

"There may have been many faster horses, no doubt many handsomer, but for bottom and endurance I never saw his fellow," praised the Duke about his warhorse.

Copenhagen died at age twenty-eight and was buried under an oak tree with military honors.

Copenhagen

Siete Leguas

Siete Leguas made Francisco "Pancho" Villa a better bandit.

The big black mare helped the Mexican revolutionary (whose real name was Doroteo Arango) make a clean getaway from rival revolutionaries by galloping twenty-one miles — roughly seven leagues — even though she'd been shot. (A league is about three miles.) Villa named her Siete Leguas, Spanish for seven leagues.

"The bullet passed through the mare cleanly, and Villa took her as his favorite horse. Supposedly, the mare had a far better fate than her master, for she lived into the early 1930s," wrote Villa's biographer Manuel A. Machado, Jr.

Villa, known as "Centaur of the North," was a fine horseman and well known as a sometimes cruel soldier. He and his forces even eluded 5,000 U.S. cavalry and infantry soldiers, led by General John J. Pershing, in the U.S. government's Punitive Expedition (1916–1917).

Villa was shot and killed in 1923 as he drove his car in Parral, Chihuahua, Mexico. He was forty-five.

Siete Leguas was Pancho Villa's favorite horse.

4 CALL TO THE POST

Racehorse athletes and their efforts to fulfill the dreams of the people who loved them are honored.

Man o' War

«(Saratoga, Aug 7ᵗʰ 1920)» Man o'War «(E. Sande - Up)»

"He's got everything a horse ought to have, and he's got it where a horse ought to have it. He's just de mostest hoss that ever drew breath."

So gushed groom Will Harbut in praise of Man o' War. No one knew him better or loved the big chestnut stallion more. They were best friends for fifteen years.

Man o' War, nicknamed Big Red, was a superstar on the racetrack and as a sire. In 1920, he won the Preakness Stakes, set an American record time of 2:14 1/5 in the one mile and three-eighths Belmont Stakes, and won the Lawrence Realization by 100 lengths. He won twenty of twenty-one races and was named Horse of the Year in 1920. He lost just once, upset by a horse named Upset in the Sanford Memorial at Saratoga on August 13, 1919.

Controversy, however, still clouds that unexpected loss. In those days, a webbing barrier served as a starting gate. The barrier sprang (Man o' War had already broken through five times, so eager was he to run); Man o' War was unprepared, maybe even facing the wrong way. The race began and Big Red scrambled to catch up. He fought through traffic and got boxed in, yet he lost to Upset by only half a length. Reports the National Museum of Racing and Hall of Fame: "Man o' War blew past Upset right after the finish line."

Man o' War showed power and passion to win the 1920 Dwyer Stakes at Aqueduct. Man o' War and John P. Grier were so formidable that all other horse owners were scared off. The Dwyer became a match race. Man o' War and John

P. Grier raced together, head to head most of the way, over the one and one-eighth mile distance. When John P. Grier nosed ahead nearing the finish line, jockey Clarence Kummer popped Man o' War with his whip. That was enough to get Man o' War to surge ahead to win by one and a half lengths and set a new American record of 1:49 1/5.

In his last race — a $75,000 match race in Windsor, Ontario (Canada) on October 12, 1920 — he cruised away from Sir Barton, the first winner of the American Triple Crown, and won by seven lengths.

"I looked back several times to see where Sir Barton was because I did not want to be surprised by a sudden burst of speed," Kummer said in a *New York Times* page-one story, "but when I reached the head of the stretch and saw that Sir Barton was several lengths back and straightened out I did not urge Man o' War. I just let him finish under restraint and had a hard time to hold his head."

Man o' War set three world records, two American records, seven track records, won $249,465, and sired sixty-four stakes winners.

He was bred by August Belmont II and named by Mrs. Belmont as she sent her husband off to World War I. A man o' war is a warship. Man o' War's Triple Crown-winning son was

Man o' War & Secretariat
THE TWENTIETH CENTURY'S TWO BIG REDS

"Both defied comparison with the best of their respective generations, and each produced a particularly spectacular performance with which they will always be identified. In Man o' War's case it was his 100-length victory in the Lawrence Realization of 1920. Secretariat, of course, entered the realm of legend with his 31-length triumph in the Belmont Stakes of 1973."

~

"People expected them to produce their own kind and that was neither fair nor possible."

~

"Two outstanding physical specimens, they filled the eye and the imaginations of those fortunate enough to have seen them race. They lived and raced half a century apart, these two Big Reds, but now they are together at last as eternal reference points for the sport."

~

"The Century's Two Greatest Horses"

JOE HIRSCH, *Daily Racing Form*, October 6, 1989
(On the occasion of Secretariat's death)

War Admiral. Another son was the history-making steeplechaser Battleship; a grandson was 1938 Horse of the Year Seabiscuit (a type of bread sailors eat).

As a yearling, Big Red was sold to Samuel D. Riddle and raced his entire career in Riddle's black-and-yellow silks.

In 1947, Will Harbut and thirty-year-old Man o' War died within one month of each other. The great horse is buried at the

Kentucky Horse Park in Lexington where his hero-sized bronze likeness welcomes visitors.

In 1999, *The Blood-Horse* magazine conducted a poll among horsemen, racing writers, and horse racing fans, asking all to vote for the best racehorse of the twentieth century. Man o' War earned the honor — "Horse of the Century." He was inducted into the National Museum of Racing's Hall of Fame in 1957.

Secretariat

"He looked like a Rolls-Royce in a field of Volkswagens," swooned Chick Lang, the former general manager of Pimlico Racetrack. He was blessed to share the air that day with Secretariat and witness the historic running of the 1973 Preakness Stakes.

Secretariat's romp to Thoroughbred racing's 1973 American Triple Crown secured his place in history and, framed in Meadow Stable's blue-and-white checkered blinkers, made him one of America's most famous faces.

During that spring campaign, which ended a twenty-five year Triple Crown drought, he set three world records that still stand today. On May 5, he clocked 1:59 2/5 in the mile and one-quarter Kentucky Derby. Showing off with speed to spare, he ran each quarter *faster* than the previous quarter! In the mile and three-sixteenths Preakness Stakes, he won by two and a half lengths, setting a record of 1:53.

Secretariat's crowning achievement came in the grueling mile-and-a-half Belmont Stakes, the longest and last jewel of the Triple Crown. He clocked 2:24 in this race on June 9 — besting his own Kentucky Derby record, running a mile and one-quarter in 1:59 — and pulverized the field, winning by thirty-one lengths. Twice A Prince, the second-place finisher, closed nearer to the last-place horse than to Secretariat.

A son of the stallion Bold Ruler and the mare Somethingroyal, Secretariat graced the covers of *Time, Newsweek,* and *Sports Illustrated.* He won sixteen of twenty-one races, was twice named Horse of the Year, and is considered the greatest racehorse of the twentieth century's second half.

"This red horse with blue and white blinkers and silks seemed to epitomize an American hero," praised Penny Chenery, who owned Secretariat with her family (and later a syndicate). He died in 1989 at age nineteen at Claiborne Farm in Kentucky, having passed on his spectacular genes to future generations of Thoroughbreds. He is buried in the farm's equine cemetery and was inducted into the National Museum of Racing's Hall of Fame in 1974.

When Secretariat died, it was discovered his heart was two and a half times larger than the heart of the average horse.

Secretariat wins the 1973 Belmont Stakes by thirty-one lengths.

Aristides

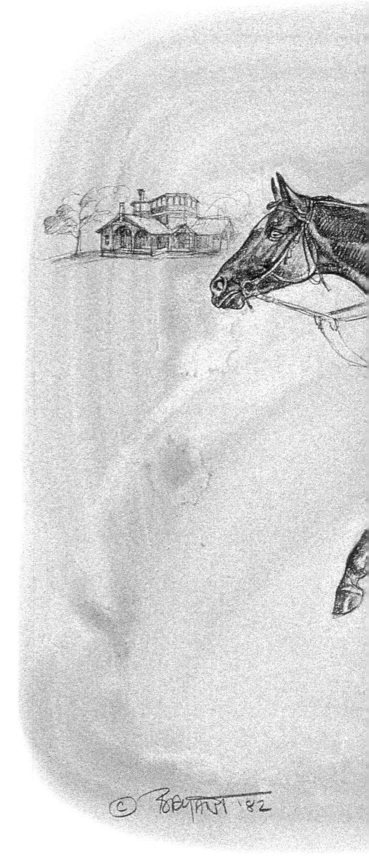

The race was one and one-half miles, the track was called Louisville Jockey Club, and a red-rose garland did not yet greet the victor to the winner's circle. But the stage was forever set for the "fastest two minutes in sports" when three-year-old Aristides won the inaugural Kentucky Derby on May 17, 1875.

It was a sunny Kentucky day — the first "Derby Day" — and the chestnut colt Aristides bested a big field of fourteen horses to win by two lengths in a record-setting time of 2:37 ¾. He was ridden by African-American jockey Oliver Lewis and carried 100 pounds.

Filling the stands, wrote John L. O'Connor, were more than 10,000 race-goers of "all grades of society, the banker, the merchant, the gentleman of leisure and pleasure seeker, the butcher, the baker, the candlestick maker…

"That portion of the Grand Stand devoted to the ladies was one grand bouquet of beauty, refinement and intelligence. The ladies in the various costumes looked like so many parti-colored butterflies…"

H. P. McGrath of Kentucky owned Aristides, who was named after Aristides Welch, owner of the colt's fine sire Leamington.

The Kentucky Derby was the brainchild of Meriwether Lewis Clark Jr., (grandson of explorer William Clark) who fashioned it after England's ever-so-fashionable Epsom Derby. Roses entered Derby tradition in 1883 when ladies received roses at a post-race party. In 1896, the race was shortened to one and one-quarter miles.

Since 1875, not one first Saturday in May has passed without the "Run for the Roses," a rite of spring for Thoroughbred three-year-olds, under the twin spires of Churchill Downs in Louisville, Kentucky.

Aristides, winner of the first Kentucky Derby, and his owner H. P. McGrath

Survivor

Horse racing in the 1800s

Two years before the first Kentucky Derby, the dream of Maryland Governor Oden Bowie became reality with the running of the first Preakness Stakes.

It was May 27, 1873 — a muggy spring Tuesday — when 12,000 racing fans gathered at Pimlico Race Course in Baltimore, Maryland, to watch seven starters vie for inaugural-Preakness bragging rights. The Maryland Jockey Club's blue-and-white pennants fluttered festively over the Victorian clubhouse and violet-painted stands.

The race was long — one and a half miles — and obliterating the field by ten lengths was the bay colt Survivor, owned by John F. Chamberlin and ridden by Englishman George Barbee.

Survivor's ten-length victory stood unchallenged for 130 years until Smarty Jones won the Preakness by eleven and a half lengths in 2004.

Why the name Preakness?

Preakness was a colt that won the 1870 Dinner Party Stakes during Pimlico's opening season. Survivor's victory came during Pimlico's first-ever spring meeting.

Today, the Preakness Stakes is run at Pimlico every third Saturday of May over a distance of one and three-sixteenths miles. It is the second jewel in American Thoroughbred racing's Triple Crown, the shortest of the three races, and is contested between the Kentucky Derby and the Belmont Stakes.

Ruthless

The mare Ruthless won the first Belmont Stakes.

A bay filly was the first to win the Belmont Stakes, the oldest of America's three Thoroughbred Triple Crown races. She enjoyed beating the boys.

Her name was Ruthless, born in 1864 to the British-bred Eclipse and the Irish mare Barbarity. She beat three colts to win the Belmont on a heavy track, June 19, 1867, at Jerome Park, in the Bronx, New York — eight years prior to the first Kentucky Derby and six years prior to the Preakness.

"Won cleverly by a head," reported a track race chart, in a time of 3:05 for the one mile and five-eighths mile race. Her owner/breeder Francis Morris collected $2,500 for the Belmont win.

At two, she won the Nursery Stakes and at three — in addition to the Belmont Stakes — she won the Spring Stakes and "the following day defeated older colts" in a mile and one-quarter race. Of eleven starts, she won seven.

The pretty mare died at twelve years old in 1876 and was inducted into the National Museum of Racing's Hall of Fame in 1975.

Sir Barton

Sir Barton loses to Man o' War in their 1920 match race.

Sir Barton won the Kentucky Derby, the Preakness Stakes, and the Belmont Stakes — the three jewels in America's Thoroughbred Triple Crown — in 1919, yet didn't get crowned until 1930. That's when *Daily Racing Form* writer Charles Hatton popularized the phrase when writing about Gallant Fox's sweep of the three classic races.

Sir Barton — a chestnut colt by Star Shoot out of Lady Sterling, by Hanover — was purchased at two by Commander J. K. L. Ross, a decorated officer in the Royal Canadian Navy. Ross paid $10,000 for him at the Saratoga horse sales and took him to his 400-acre Maryland farm.

Unheralded when stepping May 10 onto the Churchill Downs track, Sir Barton led wire to wire and won the Kentucky Derby by five lengths. Only four days later, with precious little rest, Sir Barton won the Preakness Stakes at Pimlico, winning wire to wire again, cantering in four lengths in front.

Continuing the colt's grueling campaign, trainer H. G. Bedwell and Ross shipped Sir Barton to Belmont Park, where he ran May 24 in the one-mile Withers Stakes. Again, he won. Sir Barton completed his Triple Crown coup on June 11 in the Belmont Stakes and set a track record of 2:17 2/5. In those days, the Belmont was contested at one mile and three-eighths.

"During the last eighth (jockey Johnny) Loftus sat still as a statue, holding his mount back as well as he could, but the beautiful chestnut could not be restrained entirely," reported the *New York Times*. "He was endowed with the spirit of competition and ran straight and true to the end, pulling up without showing the least trace of weariness."

At three, Sir Barton won eight races and was named champion three-year-old colt and Horse of the Year. At four, he won five races; all in all, he won more than $110,000 for Commander Ross.

Sir Barton may be best remembered for his Kenilworth Park Gold Cup match race in Canada with Man o' War on October 12, 1920. He lost by seven lengths in Man o' War's final race, though some said Sir Barton was sore. Fourteen cameras placed around the track in Windsor, Ontario, recorded the race for posterity.

Eventually, Sir Barton was sold to the U. S. Army to help breed good cavalry horses and later was purchased by Dr. J. R. Hylton of Douglas, Wyoming.

So Sir Barton — honored by the East Coast gentry as the first winner of the Triple Crown — moved West and died in Wyoming on October 30, 1937, at age twenty-one. He was inducted into the National Museum of Racing's Hall of Fame in 1957 and the Canadian Horse Racing Hall of Fame in 1976.

Red Rum

Rummy ran circles around naysayers who said it couldn't be done. No horse could do it, they said. But he did; he won the world's most grueling steeplechase three times…and sandwiched in two second-place finishes to boot. All in five years — five *consecutive* years — from 1973 to 1977.

The thirty fences, the exhausting distance of four and a half miles, Becher's Brook's towering height and precipitous drop over a "brook" of water, riderless horses with reins flapping — all create the pageantry, terror, and prestige of the Grand National, the steeplechase held every April at Aintree Racecourse near Liverpool, England.

For most, just completing "the world's greatest steeplechase" is feat enough.

Red Rum, nicknamed Rummy by his legions of fans, was born in Ireland on May 3, 1965. Early on he won a number of flat and hurdles races, and steeplechases for several owners. At about six, he began to battle a hoof disease called pedal osteitis, which affected his soundness and performances. With an uncertain future, seven-year-old Red Rum was bought by trainer Donald "Ginger" McCain for Noel Le Mare.

Serendipity smiled on the alliance. Red Rum's new home was Southport, England, a town which hugs the Lancashire seacoast. The soft sands of the beach and dunes, coupled with the swirling icy waters of the Irish Sea, worked magic on his feet. He played in the surf, galloped among the sandhills, and sprinted along the shoreline.

On the day prior to his first Grand National victory in 1973, McCain worked Rummy a mile and a half on the beach. He won by less than one length in front of the staggering and spent Crisp. In 1974, Red Rum won the National by seven lengths.

Three weeks later, McCain ran Rummy in the four-mile Scottish Grand National. He won and entered the history books as the first horse to win both races in the same year. In 1975, he placed second in the Grand National behind L'Escargot and second again in 1976 behind Rag Trade.

And so in 1977, Rummy was twelve. Could he do it again… would he be asked to? Easily asked, Rummy won over a field of forty-one horses and reigned supreme, winning by twenty-five lengths.

In the 1977 National's stretch run, Sir Peter O'Sullevan joyfully crowed on the BBC:

"He's coming up to the line to win it like a fresh horse in great style. It's hats off and a tremendous reception — you've never heard the like of it at Liverpool! Red Rum wins the National!"

That night, Rummy and McCain walked the red carpet into Southport's Bold Hotel to celebrate.

In 1978 as he prepped for his sixth Grand National, Rummy suffered a hairline fracture in a foot bone and was retired. He then had time to lead parades, make personal appearances, and graze in his pasture. Children scrambled all around and under him. Everyone wanted to pet him. He loved and was loved.

Rummy died at thirty years old and is buried near Aintree's winning post.

Red Rum on his way to winning his third Grand National Steeplechase

Phar Lap

Phar Lap arrived in Australia when the land "down under" needed a lift.

The "Aussies" (as Australians are called) were gripped in the darkness of their country's economic Great Depression. Then into their lives galloped this big red chestnut, who stood almost seventeen hands. Phar Lap offered a happy distraction and soon would reflect his name, which means "lightning" in the Thai language.

Hugh Telford bought him in 1928 as a yearling in New Zealand for the bargain-basement price of 160 guineas (about $800 in American dollars) and sent him to his brother Harry, a horse trainer in Australia. Harry Telford recruited American businessman David J. Davis to buy the racing prospect; Telford would train him.

That plan went awry at the dock when Phar Lap was unloaded. Davis didn't like him. He was lanky and lean, his face covered in warts. Davis leased him to Telford, keeping a portion of any future winnings.

At first, Davis' misgivings proved prophetic. Phar Lap was unplaced in his first four races. He won a maiden juvenile handicap (a race for young horses who've never won a race) on April 27, 1929, followed by four straight no-shows. Then a light came on for Phar Lap, and he began to race like his name.

That year he won many big races, including the Rosehill Guineas, Australian Jockey Club Derby, Australian Jockey Club Craven Plate, and Victoria Racing Club Derby. He closed out 1929 with a third in the Melbourne Cup, the highlight of every November's Melbourne Cup Carnival.

As Phar Lap's talent grew into his big body, he made a best friend — assistant trainer Tommy Woodcock, who loved him, too, and called him Bobby. They were inseparable; Phar Lap wouldn't eat if Woodcock weren't nearby.

And Phar Lap continued to win. In 1930, he won the Melbourne Stakes and three days later Australians cheered him as he captured the two-mile Melbourne Cup. During one week of the Spring Racing Carnival, Phar Lap won four races — a lot to ask of any racehorse. He won nineteen of twenty-one races that year.

The 1931 Futurity Stakes challenged Phar Lap in a different way. It was a short, seven-furlong race stocked with sprinters. Phar Lap's tremendous stride required some distance to power up. Early on he trailed by thirty lengths, then jockey Jim Pike found an opening, and they passed the pack to win. Bobby got two more nicknames: The Red Terror and Big Red.

At five, Phar Lap won eight races in Australia. In the 1931 Melbourne Cup, he carried a hefty 150 pounds and finished eighth, his last race in Australia.

Phar Lap was big news; he attracted huge crowds and won lots of money. It was a heady time for Harry Telford and Davis. Why not race him in America? But first...they committed to run him in the Agua Caliente Handicap on March 20, 1932, in Tijuana, Mexico.

Woodcock felt Phar Lap deserved a rest, but he sailed with his horse and prepped him for the Handicap. The long voyage tired Phar Lap and, though nursing a cut hoof, he won the one mile

Phar Lap is in the Australian and New Zealand Racing Halls of Fame.

and one-quarter race and set a new track record of 2:02 4/5.

Finally, Phar Lap got a break and was shipped to California.

Suddenly and shockingly, Phar Lap died on April 5, 1932, at only five. He died possibly from colic, a bacterial infection, or, as some suspected, poisoning — accidental or otherwise.

Heartsick, Harry Telford eulogized Phar Lap: "He was an angel. A human being couldn't have had more sense. He was almost human; could do anything but talk. I've never practised idolatry, but my….I loved that horse."

Phar Lap had won thirty-seven of fifty-one races and $301,402 (in American dollars), the world's second-leading money earner among Thoroughbreds at that time. He was inducted into the Australian Racing Hall of Fame in 2001, gaining legend status in 2008; and inducted into the New Zealand Racing Hall of Fame in 2006. His hide was mounted and is displayed at Melbourne Museum.

Jay Trump

Jay Trump battled Freddie over the last jump to win the 1965 Grand National.

Jay Trump battled to the finish line in England's 1965 Grand National and carried the day for a three-part, red-white-and-blue American victory. He was the first American-bred, American-owned, and American-ridden horse to win the storied steeplechase.

Born in 1957, the product of a chance mating between Tonga Prince and the mare Be Trump, he started racing on the flat at two, failing to show in four starts. At three, he ran four times, finishing second once.

About that time, amateur steeplechase rider Crompton "Tommy" Smith, Jr. — a member of a prominent Virginia fox-hunting and steeplechasing family — was sent by Mary Stephenson of Cincinnati to find her a steeplechase prospect. Tommy found Jay Trump running at a West Virginia racetrack and bought him in June 1960 for $2,000. He saw in Jay Trump what sculptors see in a slab of marble — potential. Bright, shining, sterling-silver potential. And so the big bay gelding began training over fences, ran in

steeplechase races, and hunted to hounds.

He was well known as well-mannered, intelligent, and strong of substance.

In 1963, with Smith riding, he won the Maryland Hunt Cup. In 1964, he won the My Lady's Manor, the Grand National Point-to-Point, and the Maryland Hunt Cup again.

The next year, Jay Trump shipped to England to train for his first Grand National. Waiting for him was Englishman Fred Winter, a first-year trainer and former jockey who'd won the Grand National twice. Winter knew the jumps, the dangers, and the best places to make up distance.

The big day came: April 3, 1965. Even before Smith got his "leg up" onto the saddle, he was rattled. Dressing in Aintree's jocks' room, he discovered the yellow cap cover of Mrs. Stephenson's racing silks missing. He found a black replacement cap cover, but feared Mrs. Stephenson would be angry. She wasn't mad at all; she was concerned only that Smith and Jay Trump make it safely around the four-mile, eight-hundred-and-fifty-six-yard course.

Forty-seven horses queued up at the tape — including The Rip, owned by England's Queen Mother — and broke "like a cavalry charge," Smith recalled.

Jay Trump sailed over the first five obstacles. The sixth was the frightening Becher's Brook.

"Jay Trump had never jumped a drop fence. But he jumped this one like he'd been jumping them all his life...I thought our descent would never end. It felt like his rear-end was way up in the air; that he would have to turn over when he landed. But all came out just fine, and what a thrill it was to gallop on to the seventh."

Around the Grand National course they pounded. Smith followed Winter's advice to "keep inside" and "let Jay Trump figure those fences out for himself."

Jay Trump, perhaps thinking he was back in Virginia galloping over hunt country, had things well in hand, then hit trouble. At the first fence (second time around), he landed on a fallen jockey. A few fences later, he was struck in the chest by Leedsey, a somersaulting horse. But Jay Trump kept running and jumping and Smith stayed aboard. The American pair, competing in their first Grand National, conquered Aintree's thirty fences including The Chair (the highest fence), Valentine's Brook, Canal Turn, and the precipitous Becher's Brook.

After a fight-it-out stretch duel with the Scottish horse, Freddie, victory was theirs by a length.

From England, they flew to Paris and ran in the Grand Steeple-Chase de Paris, finishing third. Then back to America, and they ran in more steeplechases and won a third Maryland Hunt Cup victory.

Jay Trump emerged from his travails a hero, the centerpiece of a story in which he made history when someone believed in him.

Sweet retirement followed and Jay Trump died in 1988 at age thirty-one. He is buried by the finish line of the Kentucky Horse Park's steeplechase course.

He was inducted into the National Museum of Racing and Hall of Fame in 1971.

Battleship, winning the Roslyn Steeplechase (Long Island, New York), 1934

Battleship

Battleship was the smallest of horses with the biggest of hearts.

He was the first American-bred and American-owned horse to win the Grand National Steeplechase at Aintree Racecourse in England, and the first to win both England's Grand National and the American Grand National.

A chestnut son of the mighty Man o' War, he was born at Mereworth Farm in 1927. At two and three, he won four of ten flat races; at four, he won six of twelve starts. Late in his fourth year, Mrs. Marion duPont Scott bought him for $12,000 and sent him into steeplechase training. In 1934, he won the American Grand National at Belmont Park.

In 1938, at eleven, Battleship prepped for the Grand National. Sitting tall in the saddle on little Battleship was six-foot, two-inch jockey Bruce Hobbs, a boy of seventeen and son of Reg Hobbs, Battleship's trainer.

Trainer Hobbs harbored fears of running Battleship in Britain's grueling Grand National.

"She's a lovely person, the owner, but she must be mighty tough to even think of running this dear little horse over Aintree," lamented Hobbs on the race's eve. "He's only 15.2, too small to see over the Chair Fence, let alone Becher's…"

His fears turned to elation when Battleship, nicknamed "The American Pony," stuck his nose out at the finish to beat Royal Danieli and win.

Battleship sired fifty-eight foals — nineteen percent were stakes winners — and steeplechase champions War Battle and Shipboard, and 1952 American Grand National winner Sea Legs.

Battleship lived out his thirty-one years on Mrs. Scott's grand Montpelier estate in Virginia. He was inducted into the National Museum of Racing's Hall of Fame in 1969.

Citation

Citation, with jockey Eddie Arcaro and trainer Jimmy Jones

Citation was the first millionaire Thoroughbred.

Before achieving that figure, he set another benchmark in 1948 when he won Thoroughbred racing's American Triple Crown — the Kentucky Derby, Preakness Stakes, and Belmont Stakes. Twenty-five years passed until Secretariat did it again in 1973.

Citation was a blueblood, bred and born at Kentucky's Calumet Farm, a son of Bull Lea. His dam was the British imported mare Hydroplane II, a daughter of Hyperion.

A big bay with large, expressive eyes, he was called an efficient runner, a get-down-to-business horse. In 1948, he and jockey Eddie Arcaro had won the Kentucky Derby and the Preakness. The Triple Crown was theirs if they could win the Belmont on June 12.

Wearing the No. 1A saddlecloth, Citation bolted from the gate then stumbled, nearly pitching Arcaro off. That Arcaro stayed aboard and that Citation recovered to conquer the field by more than half a dozen lengths are testament to the talents of both. In the Belmont, they equaled the stakes record of 2:28 1/5 for one and one-half miles.

"He's the greatest horse I've ever seen. Maybe I shouldn't have let him win by so much, but I couldn't take any chances for that kind of money. I think he can run an eighth in 0:11 flat in any part of any race," Arcaro said.

Citation capped his career on July 14, 1951, by winning the Hollywood Gold Cup and $100,000, pushing his earnings to $1,085,760. He won thirty-two of forty-five races.

Citation died at age twenty-five at home on Calumet Farm, where he is buried.

He was named Horse of the Year in 1948 and inducted into the National Museum of Racing's Hall of Fame in 1959.

Seabiscuit

Seabiscuit and jockey George Woolf on a morning workout

Seabiscuit's gift to America mirrored Phar Lap's gift to Australia. He taught a country in crisis that better days can come by sheer will. He was a beacon of hope — a brightener, a distraction, a hero — during America's dark days of the Great Depression.

Bred by Gladys Phipps' Wheatley Stable, foaled in 1933, he was a son of Hard Tack and grandson of the mighty Man o' War. His dam was Swing On, by Whisk Broom II.

The bay Thoroughbred grew up in top-class company at Claiborne Farm. At two, Seabiscuit began running on the East Coast in claiming races and won his first race on June 22, 1935, at

Seabiscuit (continued)

Narragansett Park. That fall, he won the Springfield Handicap at Agawam Park in Massachusetts and the Ardsley Handicap at Empire City Racetrack in New York.

Tom Smith, trainer for wealthy Californian Charles Howard, saw Seabiscuit race one June day in 1936 in Boston. When Smith and Howard saw him win at Saratoga in August, they bought him for $8,000.

At three, Seabiscuit won three big handicap races in the East and by November was in California, where he won the Bay Bridge and World's Fair handicaps at Bay Meadows. He was winning and loving it.

Seabiscuit started his four-year-old season by losing by a nose the Santa Anita Handicap with its winner-take-all prize of $100,000, then set the country's racetracks afire, crisscrossing America by train. He won nine handicaps and the Laurel Stakes in Maryland. By the end of 1937, he was America's top Thoroughbred money winner, earning almost $168,000.

Early in 1938, with Seabiscuit atop the racing world, regular jockey Red Pollard was injured in a racing spill (not aboard Seabiscuit) and replaced by George Woolf. In February, they lost the Hundred-Grander again by a nose. But he rolled on and won the Agua Caliente Handicap in Mexico and the Bay Meadows Handicap a second time.

Sensing a publicity coup, officials at Belmont Park in New York arranged a match race for May between Seabiscuit — the West Coast champion — and 1937 Triple Crown winner War Admiral, darling of the East Coast. The prospect of his horse defeating War Admiral tantalized Howard. But plans fell through when Seabiscuit injured his left front tendon.

Seabiscuit recovered to win the Hollywood Gold Cup, a match race at Del Mar, and the Havre de Grace Handicap in Maryland. In July, Pollard was injured yet again, suffering a catastrophic leg injury in a barn accident. Woolf remained Seabiscuit's jockey.

On November 1 the big match race with War Admiral materialized. The Pimlico Special was run over one and one-sixteenth miles at Pimlico Race Course in Baltimore.

Forty-thousand people crowded the track; thousands more listened to the race call on radio. People crushed by uncertainty, with World War II looming, forgot their woes for at least that afternoon.

War Admiral was favored, Seabiscuit was unafraid. In fact, Seabiscuit and War Admiral were related. In human terms, they were half-brothers. Man o' War sired War Admiral and Hard Tack; Hard Tack sired Seabiscuit. Seabiscuit and War Admiral both were smallish, standing just above fifteen hands.

"The Admiral looked Seabiscuit in the eye at the three-quarters (pole) but Seabiscuit never got the look. He was too busy running, with his shorter, faster stride.

"For almost a half mile they ran as one horse, painted against the green, red and orange foliage of a Maryland countryside. They were neck and neck — head and head — nose and nose," wrote Grantland Rice in *The Baltimore Sun.* "(War Admiral) had never before met a combination of a grizzly bear and a running fool." Seabiscuit beat his relative by four lengths and set a track record.

Fortunes soon changed. Seabiscuit's left front tendon ruptured, and he and Pollard convalesced together at Howard's Ridgewood Ranch in California.

In 1940, when Seabiscuit was seven, Pollard guided him to victory – finally! — in the mile and one-quarter Hundred-Grander, running in a huge field of thirteen, and set a new track record of 2:01 1/5. Seabiscuit was retired to Ridgewood and sired 108 foals.

Seabiscuit was 1937 champion male handicap horse and 1938 Horse of the Year. In eighty-nine races, he won thirty-three; placed second fifteen times; and ran third thirteen times. He died on May 17, 1947, after winning $437,730 on the track. The little horse with the big heart set sixteen track records.

Seabiscuit was inducted into the National Museum of Racing's Hall of Fame in 1958.

Seattle Slew

The 1970s produced a bumper crop of Triple Crown champions.

During that single decade, three colts won the American Triple Crown of horse racing — the Kentucky Derby, the Preakness Stakes, and the Belmont Stakes. It hadn't been done before and it hasn't been done since. Secretariat won in 1973, Seattle Slew in 1977, and Affirmed in 1978.

(Continued on next page)

Seattle Slew

Seattle Slew (continued)

Winning Thoroughbred racing's Triple Crown is one of the most difficult feats in all of sports. Only the tenth horse in history to win the coveted honor, Seattle Slew was the first to capture the crown with an unbeaten record (six undefeated starts).

He was called the "bargain horse" because he was purchased for only $17,500 at a Kentucky yearling sale by Mickey and Karen Taylor. (Paying hundreds of thousands of dollars, even millions, is not uncommon for Thoroughbreds with blue-ribbon breeding.)

Sharing partnership of Seattle Slew were veterinarian Dr. James Hill and his wife Sally. Slew's name derived from the Taylors' home near Seattle and the sloughs (pools of water) of south Florida, where Dr. Hill grew up. Karen Taylor preferred the spelling of "slew" to "sloughs" and the Taylors and Hills became known as "The Slew Crew."

A high-spirited, dark-brown colt, Slew was born in 1974, a son of Bold Reasoning and great-grandson of Bold Ruler, Secretariat's sire. He was smart, headstrong, and known to plow through competitors who crowded him.

On September 16, 1978, Slew and Affirmed made history again in the Marlboro Cup at Belmont Park. It was the only time two Triple Crown winners had raced each other. Seattle Slew won by three lengths over the one-year younger Affirmed.

Slew won fourteen of seventeen races. He was a fighter off the track as well, battling through two spinal surgeries and a viral infection that nearly killed him at four.

"If Seattle Slew was human, he'd be Muhammad Ali," said Angel Cordero, Jr., one of his jockeys. "Jumping, strutting, and cocky, but good — the best horse I've ever been on."

He was champion two-year-old male in 1976, champion three-year-old male in 1977, Horse of the Year in 1977, champion handicap horse at four years old, and 1984's leading sire. He won more than $1.2 million.

Slew retired in Kentucky in 1979 and was as talented at passing along his good genes as he was at racing. He sired more than 100 stakes winners and superior broodmares. He died peacefully in 2002 at age twenty-eight, twenty-five years to the day that he won the 1977 Kentucky Derby. The Taylors were with him.

"A very special horse, the love of our lives from the beginning," eulogized Karen Taylor. "We were lucky to be his caretakers here on earth."

Slew was inducted into the National Museum of Racing's Hall of Fame in 1981.

Seattle Slew

Affirmed

One of the greatest rivalries in sports history pitted two chestnut Thoroughbred colts against each other — Affirmed and Alydar — in down-to-the-wire duels in the 1978 American Triple Crown races: the Kentucky Derby, the Preakness Stakes, and the Belmont Stakes.

Affirmed won each classic race by diminishing distances over Alydar: the Derby (May 6, Churchill

(Continued on next page)

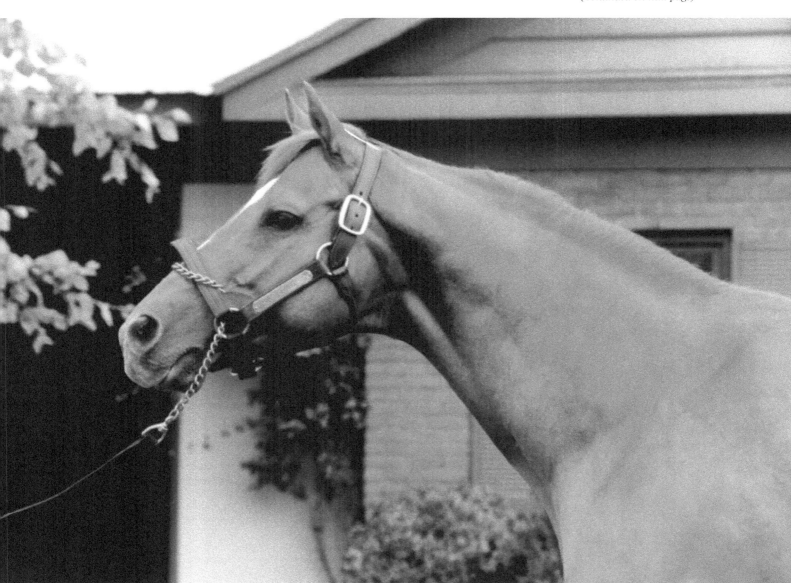

Affirmed

Affirmed (continued)

Downs, Louisville, Kentucky) by a length and a half; the Preakness (May 20, Pimlico Race Course, Baltimore, Maryland) by a neck; and the Belmont Stakes (June 10, Belmont Park, Elmont, New York) by a head.

Riding Affirmed in the three classic races was teenage wunderkind Steve Cauthen, all of eighteen years old.

In the Belmont Stakes' stretch run, with the Triple Crown at stake, Affirmed and Alydar ran so tightly together that Cauthen changed his whip from his right hand to his left. With this last encouragement on his left hip, Affirmed thrust forward to win by a head.

"I wasn't worried about any other horse in the race," Cauthen said later. "I knew that Alydar would come up and we would fight it out. I didn't think we'd have to fight it out for a mile, but with Affirmed and Alydar, it always seems to turn out that they fight for every inch. I wanted the first part of the race to be slow because the last part was going to be very fast."

Affirmed's official Belmont time was 2:26 4/5.

The two dashing colts met ten times during their racing careers. Affirmed won seven of those meetings; Alydar won three.

Their final showdown was the Travers Stakes on August 19, 1978, at Saratoga Race Course in New York. Affirmed easily won, but fouled Alydar on the far turn and was moved to second, giving up the victory to Alydar. In the fall of 1979, Affirmed capped his career (without Alydar in either field) by winning the Woodward Stakes and the Jockey Club Gold Cup at Belmont.

Affirmed's sire was Exclusive Native. He was bred and owned by Louis and Patrice Wolfson and trained by Laz Barrera. He won almost $2.4 million — the first North American Thoroughbred to surpass the $2 million mark. He was named champion two-year-old male in 1977; Horse of the Year in 1978 and 1979; champion three-year-old male in 1978; and champion older male in 1979.

Alydar's trainer, John Veitch, praised Affirmed: "He had the speed to get out front and the heart to hold off challengers."

Affirmed died at age twenty-six in Kentucky and was inducted into the National Museum of Racing's Hall of Fame in 1980.

Smuggler

The next time you pass a horse barn — whether it be modest or grand — look up and you might see Smuggler twirling in the wind.

Smuggler was a Kansas-bred, white-faced stallion and hero of 1870s harness racing, one of America's first spectator sports. On September 15, 1874, Smuggler raced at Mystic Park in the Boston suburb of Medford, for title of the "Fastest Trotting Stallion in the United States." Forty-thousand fans watched him win the victor's $10,000 purse.

Smuggler was honored with a copper weather vane, produced by Boston's Harris and Company and W. A. Snow Company. Reproductions abound on rooftops, in antique shops, and as horsey décor in retail shops.

Smuggler graces the roofs of many stables.

Dan Patch

A master of marketing was a champion pacer named Dan Patch.

His image graced postcards, cooking stoves, a railroad line, washing machines, and clocks. He traveled in his own private train car. As children, future presidents Harry Truman wrote him a fan letter and Dwight D. Eisenhower watched him race at the Kansas State Fair.

He set an early standard for America's sport superstars.

The mahogany-brown stallion was born in 1896 in Oxford, Indiana, bred by Dan Messner, Jr., who named him "Dan" after himself and "Patch" after his sire, Joe Patchen. In 1902, wealthy Minnesotan Marion W. Savage bought him for $60,000.

At the 1906 Minnesota State Fair, 93,000 fans watched Dan Patch set the one-mile record of 1:55, a record that stood for decades but not officially recorded because the sulky pulled by the pacesetter had a windshield, which was disallowed. He did set a recognized record in 1905 when he paced a mile in 1:55 ¼ in Lexington, Kentucky. He set nine world records, twenty-two state records in fourteen states and Canada, never lost a race, and was inducted into the Harness Racing Hall of Fame in 1953.

"Dan Patch at $60,000 was the cheapest horse I ever bought and he has paid for himself inside three years and could not be purchased of me for $180,000, which I was offered," said Savage.

The town of Hamilton, Minnesota, was renamed Savage to honor Dan Patch's owner. Minnesota's Dan Patch Historical Society celebrates "Dan Patch Days" every summer; Oxford, Indiana, hosts its own "Dan Patch Days" in autumn. In 1995, the main street of the Minnesota State Fairgrounds was christened "Dan Patch Avenue."

Horse and owner, a formidable team in life, dovetailed in death as well. In 1916, they died within thirty-two hours of each other, their funerals held at the same hour.

Dan Patch leads in a training session, circa 1905.

Gallant Man

Gallant Man loses the 1957 Kentucky Derby to Iron Liege in the famous "Bad Dream Derby."

The 1957 Kentucky Derby was a sorry-it-was-my-fault upset loss for jockey Bill Shoemaker. Shoemaker and Gallant Man were leading the nine-horse field on a cold and windy first Saturday in May, about seventy yards from a Kentucky Derby win and red roses in the winner's circle. Then Shoemaker mistook the sixteenth pole for the finish and stood in his stirrups. Instantly realizing his mistake, he sank back down, frantically trying to recover. But Gallant Man had lost his stride enough to lose the storied race by a nose to Iron Liege, a bay colt owned by Calumet Farm.

Shoemaker lamented after the race: "I stood up for an instant, then realized my error and went back to work. I had to get after him at the five-eighths pole. I dug into him good and the way we were moving, I thought I had it won. He's a good trying horse. However, there wasn't any question in my mind that we were second; I didn't need the camera to tell me that."

Oddly, Ralph Lowe — Gallant Man's owner — saw it coming. He dreamed of the very thing that happened and told Gallant Man's trainer, John Nerud. Lowe might have wished he hadn't shared. Nerud re-told the dream to Shoemaker on Derby eve.

The Churchill Downs crowd of 90,000 watched the prophecy fulfilled and this Kentucky Derby became known as the "Bad Dream Derby." There hadn't been a down-to-the-wire, win-by-a-nose Derby finish in twenty-four years.

Gallant Man was inducted into the National Museum of Racing's Hall of Fame in 1987.

Special Effort

Special Effort wins the 1981 All-American Futurity and the Triple Crown of Quarter Horse racing.

Special Effort was the first horse to win the Triple Crown for two-year-old Quarter Horses, winning the Kansas Futurity, the Rainbow Futurity, and the All American Futurity in 1981, racing in the red-white-and-blue silks of Dan and Jolene Urschel of Canadian, Texas.

A stunning sorrel born in 1979, he was sired by the Thoroughbred Raise Your Glass.

Special Effort won thirteen of fourteen races and more than $1.2 million. He was named World Champion for 1981, as well as champion two-year-old and champion two-year-old stallion. At three, he won the Kansas Derby, finished third in the All American Derby, and was retired to father future generations of fast Quarter Horses.

Special Effort's performance as a sire rivaled his performance as a racehorse. He fathered 1,834 foals which won almost $19 million on the track and a host of blue ribbons at halter and in the show ring, boasted Registers of Merit, regional and world championships, and included six world champions.

Special Effort died in 2006 at the age of twenty-seven and is buried on the famed 6666 Ranch in Texas. He was inducted into the American Quarter Horse Hall of Fame in 2008.

American Pharoah

It took almost four decades, thirty-seven years, but finally…a Triple Crown winner. It'd been a long wait since the wondrous 1970s, when three horses captured the Triple Crown of American Thoroughbred racing: Secretariat (1973); Seattle Slew (1977); and Affirmed (1978).

American Pharoah won the Kentucky Derby in a field of eighteen in 2015. He won the Preakness Stakes, the Triple Crown's "middle jewel," in a field of eight on a sloppy track. The mile-and-one-half Belmont Stakes was run on June 6. He won by 5 1/2 lengths in a time of 2:26 3/5. The drought was over.

After securing the crown for owner Ahmed Zayat and trainer Bob Baffert, jockey Victor Espinoza, then forty-two, relished his victory as he took American Pharoah on a victory lap to the end of the grandstand. The bay colt handled himself with grace as photos with legions of well-wishers were taken.

Espinoza had failed twice before to win the Belmont and capture the Triple Crown.

"The third time was a charm. There are (now) twelve Triple Crown winners and I have twelve brothers and sisters," he said after the race.

The colt won more than $8.5 million and was named 2015 Horse of the Year, 2015 champion three-year-old male, and 2014 champion two-year-old male.

And what of his misspelled name? Supposedly a Missouri woman entered Zayat Stables' contest to name two-year-olds from its 2014 crop. She suggested American Pharoah. (A pharaoh — not pharoah — is an Egyptian king.) Zayat Stables' owner is Egyptian, and one colt's sire was Pioneerof the Nile, a spelling anomaly to satisfy The Jockey Club's eighteen-character maximum name length. The name won, and The Jockey Club registered it.

American Pharoah won the Breeders' Cup Classic and was retired to father new generations of champion Thoroughbreds.

American Pharoah, with jockey Victor Espinoza, wins the 147th Belmont Stakes, becoming the twelfth Triple Crown winner.

Black Gold

Black Gold wins the 50th Kentucky Derby.

Black Gold might have liked to be remembered as winning the Golden Derby of 1924, the 50th Kentucky Derby.

But history recalls his guts and gallantry — his left front "hoof (dangling) as on a thread" — finishing his last race on three legs.

(Continued on next page)

Black Gold (continued)

Bedeviled by hoof and leg problems, Black Gold would not quit. Ever. And, so said some racetrackers, neither would Black Gold's trainer Hanley Webb. Warnings from blacksmiths, veterinarians, jockeys, and horsemen who noticed a limp went unheeded. Black Gold was trained and raced until he could give no more.

His dam, a little mare named Useeit, was purchased by Oklahoman Al Hoots in trade for eighty acres of land. She and Hoots won thirty-four races, then both were ruled forever off racing when Hoots refused to give her up in a claiming race.

No matter. As Hoots neared death, he dreamed of breeding Useeit to a top stallion in hopes the union would produce a Kentucky Derby champion. Useeit shipped to Kentucky — the cradle of Thoroughbred racing — and was bred to Black Toney at fashionable Idle Hour Stock Farm.

Hoots died in 1920; the colt he dreamed of arrived in early 1921. Hoots' widow, Rosa, named the foal Black Gold, a two-part tribute to his ebony coat and the oil gushing up in Oklahoma.

Black Gold debuted at the Fair Grounds in New Orleans on January 8, 1923, and won his first race. "The Black Streak" went on to win the Kentucky, Louisiana, Chicago, and Ohio derbies, eighteen of thirty-five starts, and $110,588.50.

On January 18, 1928, Webb entered Black Gold in the one-mile Salome Purse at the Fair Grounds. Black Gold was making his move toward home when, at the top of the stretch, his left foreleg snapped above the ankle. Only a bandage bound the leg together. Jockey Dave Emery tried desperately to pull him up, but Black Gold wouldn't stop until he crossed the finish line. He was euthanized quickly.

"That Black Gold possessed an abundance of courage, speed and endurance back in 1924 when he swept through the Derbies at Jefferson Park, Churchill Downs, Maple Heights and Washington Park is certain," wrote Al Tauzier for *The New Orleans Item*. "Only one of these qualities was retained at the close of his career — courage, and plenty of it. No gamer racer ever trod a track than Black Gold…"

Black Gold's life ended at age seven in New Orleans, where his racing career began. The great battler was buried in the infield. Though smallish, standing shorter than sixteen hands, he boasted the heart of a lion. Today, the winning jockey of the annual Black Gold Stakes presents flowers at his grave marker.

Black Gold was inducted into the National Museum of Racing's Hall of Fame in 1989.

Cannonade

The winner of the 100th Kentucky Derby on May 4, 1974, was the bay colt Cannonade.

The colt — owned and bred by industrialist John M. Olin, trained by Woody Stephens, and ridden by Angel Cordero Jr. — moved to the inside and powered up into high gear on the final turn, besting the huge "Run for the Roses" field of twenty-three at Churchill Downs. Prophetically carrying the No. 1 saddle cloth, Cannonade won by two and one-fourth lengths in front of a record crowd of 163,628.

"This was beautiful — all the way. Just beautiful. The horse was good. The fans were good," said Cordero.

Cannonade, a grandson of the prodigious Bold Ruler, retired at Gainesway Farm in Kentucky and died at an aged twenty-two years. His son, Caveat, won the Thoroughbred classic race, the Belmont Stakes, in 1983.

Cannonade wins the 100th Kentucky Derby.

Devon Loch belly flops on the stretch just feet from winning the 1956 Grand National.

Devon Loch

The greatest conundrum in horse-racing history is Devon Loch's belly-flop fall in England's 1956 Grand National.

And they were going so well. Jockey Dick Francis had guided the ten-year-old bay over Aintree's thirty fences — twice over the treacherous Becher's Brook; they were galloping happily down the homestretch. Only fifty yards from winning the world's most-famous steeplechase, Devon Loch fell, spread-eagled, flat on the track.

The crowd of 20,000 gasped a collective "Oh no!!" No one was more shocked than Devon Loch's owner, HM Queen Elizabeth, the Queen Mother. There had been no hint of pending disaster, no premonition of trouble, no wobbling, no signs of fatigue. A total collapse followed total domination of this Grand National.

Francis wrote about those glorious moments with victory almost theirs: "Never before in the National had I held back a horse and said 'Steady, boy.' Never had I felt such power in reserve, such confidence in my mount, such calm in my mind."

Sundry theories were put forth: Devon Loch jumped a shadow; he thought he was jumping the wing of a water jump; he shied at the grandstand noise; a simple stumble; lack of oxygen; too much glucose; a cramp. Could Devon Loch have mistaken a wet spot on the ground for a jump? The cause remains a mystery.

Devon Loch stood up, his jockey dismounted. The great opportunity lost. A track veterinarian found Devon Loch to be in perfect health afterward.

Francis later blamed the "tremendous noise" for frightening Devon Loch. He quit race riding and became a best-selling author of mysteries. Devon Loch died at the royal residence Sandringham in 1962.

Justify

Justify, with jockey Mike Smith, after winning the 150th Belmont Stakes and becoming the thirteenth Triple Crown winner.

Justify proved that lightning can strike twice.

Bob Baffert, the Hall of Fame trainer of 2015 Triple Crown winner American Pharoah, was so overwhelmed with that victory that he felt it truly was a once-in-a-lifetime joy. Never to happen again.

"Just listening to the crowd that last hundred yards was amazing. I'll probably never experience anything like this again," Baffert said after American Pharoah's victory.

Yet, it did happen to Baffert, a former Quarter Horse trainer from Arizona, in three years' time and four Triple Crown seasons. Winning the Triple Crown — the most difficult feat in Thoroughbred horse racing — is a trial that has broken many hearts since Sir Barton first won in 1919.

Justify won the 150th Belmont Stakes wire-to-wire on June 9, 2018, and sealed his place in history as the thirteenth Triple Crown winner. He is only the second horse to win the Triple Crown undefeated; Seattle Slew was the first in 1977. Baffert is only the second trainer to win two Triple Crowns, following James "Sunny Jim" Fitzsimmons in the 1930s.

Hall of Fame jockey Mike Smith, then fifty-two, rode the powerful chestnut colt in all three of Justify's Triple Crown races and in five of his six total career starts. Smith, over the moon with joy at the victory, was effusively thankful.

"He's so gifted; he was sent from heaven," said Smith. After crossing the finish line and winning horse racing's most coveted prize, Smith took Justify to the clubhouse turn for a private moment, a chance to gather his emotions. Then, in a bow to the crowd, he rode Justify to the end of the expansive Belmont grandstand, a sort-of victory lap — just as Victor Espinoza had done on American Pharoah in 2015.

Justify won by 1 3/4 lengths in a time of 2:28.18.

The Kentucky-bred colt is sired by Scat Daddy, out of Stage Magic by Ghostzapper. He won six races in 112 days and a slew of 2018 honors.

5 CELEBRITY STATUS

These horses and ponies found fame because of their special talents, famous owners, and wanderlust.

Manitou

Manitou and Theodore Roosevelt ride the Badlands of Dakota Territory.

Manitou was balm for a broken heart.

Theodore Roosevelt, an aristocratic New Yorker boasting Harvard credentials and a famous name, reveled in life's adventures, his every enterprise fueled by a "can-do" spirit. He wrote dozens of books about many subjects, including animals, naval strategy, and the American West. He nurtured passions for hunting and shooting and a constant curiosity.

Then, on one single day, his life turned upside down. Manitou helped him right his ship.

The first of a trio of tragedies happened in 1878: Nineteen-year-old TR was away studying at Harvard College when his beloved father died. Life brightened when, two years later, he married Alice Lee of Chestnut Hill, Massachusetts, and in 1881 he was elected to the New York State Assembly.

With his personal and political lives gleaming like newly minted copper pennies, the cruelest of coincidences befell young Roosevelt. On Valentine's Day 1884, his wife and his mother died within hours of each other, in the same house. Alice, twenty-two, died of kidney disease, two days after delivering a daughter; his mother, of typhoid fever.

TR sought solace in the rugged cowboy life offered in the Badlands of Dakota Territory, hunting, calving, riding the range. He thought he might outrun his grief. "Black care rarely sits behind a rider whose pace is fast enough."

Manitou provided the comfort and companionship required for Roosevelt's recovery.

"My own hunting-horse, Manitou, is the best and most valuable animal on the ranch. He is stoutly built and strong, able to carry a good-sized buck behind his rider for miles at a lope without minding it in the least; he is… enduring…very hardy…perfectly sure-footed. Though both willing and spirited, he is very gentle, with an easy mouth…and will allow a man to shoot off his back or right by him without moving, and it is evident that he is as nearly perfect as can be the case with hunting-horseflesh."

Manitou and Roosevelt roamed the Badlands and explored along the Little Missouri River. "Manitou is a treasure, and I value him accordingly."

Roosevelt returned to the East, married again, led his Rough Riders up Cuba's San Juan Hill in 1898, and at forty-two was sworn in as America's youngest president (after the assassination of President William McKinley).

Will Rogers on Teddy performs a "crinoline" rope trick at a baseball game in Boston, June 1910.

Teddy

An Oklahoma cowboy needs a good Oklahoma horse. And philosopher-humorist Will Rogers wanted Teddy.

Rogers roped horses, steers, cats, and cowboys. He could rope anything that moved, his rope an extension of his arm. In 1896, when he was seventeen, Rogers left Indian Territory (christened Oklahoma in 1907) to work on a Texas ranch. But he found no romance in ranching. He wanted adventure.

So, armed with wanderlust and a travel trunk of rope tricks, Rogers spent his early adulthood touring the world, working as a trick rider and performer in a circus, a Wild West show, anywhere he could.

Rogers began to add down-home comments about politics, people, and world events to his act and discovered that vaudeville (theater shows featuring a variety of acts) was the perfect showcase for his "all I know is just what I read in the papers" commentary.

Meanwhile, a little bay cow pony toiled at workaday chores on the Mulhall Ranch in Oklahoma, oblivious that his world was about to change from sheltered to showbiz.

Rogers' musings — accented with a drawl and bad grammar — were entertaining, but he wanted something more for his act. He'd roped horses a million ways: by the nose, the tail, with two and three ropes. Roping a running horse on stage…now THAT hadn't been done before.

He knew the horse who could do it; one calm on the stage, able to start and stop on a dime, and bright enough to obey voice commands. Rogers went home, paid $100 for the little bay, and named him Teddy after Col. Theodore Roosevelt. Rogers and Teddy debuted in New York in 1905.

Teddy galloped across slick stages wearing felt boots. He stopped on cue. Stood stock still in the footlights for Rogers' "crinoline" rope trick, when Rogers, sitting in his saddle, spun a rope until its entire 100-foot length looped low over the orchestra. Rogers and Teddy then backed up, the rope crashed onto the stage, Rogers whooped cowboy style, and they dashed into the stage wings.

Rogers said that Teddy could "do on a slick stage just about what a good turning cowpony can do on the ground."

Teddy even helped Rogers advertise their act, parading about town wearing a dark-blue blanket monogrammed with Will Rogers. He was willing when Rogers wanted action and traveled all over America and to Europe three times.

Rogers famously quipped: "I have always said I never met a man I dident like." Perhaps it was so with horses, too: "A man that don't love a horse, there is something the matter with him."

Teddy retired in 1910 and lived out a long life back on the ranch in Oklahoma.

Macaroni

Macaroni and Caroline Kennedy tour the south lawn of the White House, Washington, D.C., March 1962.

Macaroni the pony squired about the princess of Camelot.

Caroline Kennedy, daughter of President John F. Kennedy and his wife, Jacqueline, learned to ride on Macaroni, a registered Galiceno gelding sporting four white stockings and a star.

Before being thrust into the world of celebrity, he was a Texan, bred by Texas Governor John B. Connally, born in the little town Floresville, and named Little John. A gift from Vice President Lyndon B. Johnson (also a Texan), Macaroni was a frequent guest at the White House, though he lived full-time on the family farm in Virginia.

The thousand days when the Kennedys occupied the White House are often called Camelot, the fictional, idyllic English kingdom led by the heroic King Arthur.

Burmese

Early on June 13, 1981, Burmese was well into her beauty treatment. Her coat was curried to a black-satin sheen, her hooves polished to a brilliant gloss, and those little chin hairs properly trimmed — from forelock to fetlock she was spit-and-polish perfect. A big day was ahead, and Burmese knew it.

By 11 a.m., Burmese and Queen Elizabeth II of Great Britain would headline the centuries-old British ceremony called Trooping the Colour. Marching bands, musicians on horseback, hundreds of military horses, and thousands of soldiers perform every June for the Queen, Colonel-in-Chief of the seven Regiments of the Household Division. She and Burmese will walk from Buckingham Palace down The Mall and into Horse Guards Parade grounds to hold court over one of Great Britain's grandest spectacles.

The Trooping recreates the military exercise when a mounted soldier "trooped" (carried) a battalion's flag ("colour") so soldiers could identify their units on the battlefield. The Queen reviews the soldiers marching in formation, they troop the Colour, she is saluted, and she returns the salute. (The Trooping does double duty as

(Continued on next page)

Burmese makes her Trooping the Colour debut in London, 1969.

Burmese (continued)

the Queen's Birthday Parade.)

That summer of 1981, the eyes of the world were on London, a city abuzz about the royal wedding. Prince Charles, heir to the British throne, and Lady Diana Spencer would marry the next month in St. Paul's Cathedral. Lady Diana arrived by carriage at the parade grounds to watch the Trooping.

Burmese and the Queen departed the Royal Mews, which is Buckingham Palace's stable complex that houses horses and carriages, and began the journey of less than a mile, buoyed along by legions of well-wishers — smiling, laughing, and waving Union Jack flags.

Suddenly, the celebration turned to terror. A teenaged boy stepped from the crowd, aimed a pistol at Burmese and Queen Elizabeth, and fired six shots. Burmese shied slightly, soldiers ran to assist, the crowd gasped. Both were unhurt, but…did someone just try to shoot the Queen?

Drawing on a lifetime of riding and loving horses, the Queen knew just what to do. She stroked Burmese's neck, spoke to her, they caught their breaths, and on went the Trooping. The crisis was theirs and theirs alone to handle. (As it turned out, the firearm was a starting pistol, the shots were blanks, and the assailant went to jail.)

⁓

Burmese was born in 1962 in the Cypress Hills of Saskatchewan, Canada, the result of the Royal Canadian Mounted Police's carefully crafted equine breeding program. Her sire was the black Thoroughbred Faux Pas, and her dam was a specially selected broodmare named Minx. The RCMP bought and imported Faux Pas, a champion racehorse and winner at the Ascot Racecourse, in 1955 from England.

Like her parents, the little filly was blessed with raven-black beauty, brains, and style. As she grew up, these qualities made her a RCMP rising star. Corporal Ken Downey was her "remount" (young horse) trainer. He taught her the basics — as well as the finer points — of carrying a rider, mounted police duties, maneuvers required for performing in the Musical Ride, and enjoyment of her work.

The Musical Ride is a world-famous spectacle of RCMP riders and horses performing intricate drills to music and cavalry-based maneuvers. Burmese rose to the No. 1 position in the Musical Ride. When the chance arose for the RCMP to give a horse to Queen Elizabeth — the sovereign of Canada — Burmese was selected from about 75 candidates. Sgt. /Staff Sgt. Fred Rasmussen, who retired from the RCMP as Riding Master, trained her for Royal Family service.

In April 1969, Burmese and other Musical Ride horses, riders, and staff boarded a plane bound for England. The Ride performed for the Queen at Windsor Castle and on April 18, Burmese was officially presented to Queen Elizabeth.

The Queen hoped to ride Burmese in the next Trooping. But Burmese had never been ridden with a side-saddle. Lessons began.

"It made no difference to her," said Riding Master Ralph Cave. He watched Burmese's Trooping debut from a ring-side seat as a special guest of the Queen. "The shiny black mare from the Prairies was on the most important ride of her life," he said, proudly remembering the moment.

Burmese performed with grace and class in every Trooping, from 1969 until 1986, for eighteen consecutive years.

She "became the perfect lady's horse," recalled Rasmussen, today of Tofield, Alberta, Canada. "She was the right size with the right temperament…smaller than some of the (RCMP) horses…(but) very spirited and well-behaved."

Photos of Burmese and Queen Elizabeth brightened postcards, magazine covers (including *People*, on January 26, 1987), and postage stamps. The royal art collection features a bronze statue of Burmese.

When her royal duties ended, Burmese retired to Windsor Castle. She died in 1990 at age twenty-eight and was buried near the castle.

"Burmese was a kind and gentle animal anyone would love to ride… (an) elegant little black mare," praised Rasmussen.

Brigham

The Legend of the Westerner at the National Cowboy & Western Heritage Museum, in Oklahoma City, features Brigham and "Buffalo Bill."

Frontiersman William F. Cody might have missed out on fame and friendships with the royal, rich, and political if Brigham hadn't helped with a nickname.

Cody boasted a colorful resume — Pony Express rider at fifteen; stagecoach and cattle driver; scout for the Union during the Civil War and for the Fifth Cavalry on the Great Plains.

But Cody made his name when the Kansas Pacific Railroad began building tracks across Kansas in the mid-1860s. Needing to feed 1,200 workers, the railroad hired Cody to kill twelve buffaloes a day for pay of $500 per month.

Cody bought a horse from a Ute Indian and named him Brigham after Mormon leader Brigham Young. Riding the swift and smart Brigham, Cody shot more than 4,000 buffalo in seventeen months, and the railroad workers dubbed him "Buffalo Bill."

Brigham "understood everything," Cody wrote. "…and all that he expected of me was to do the shooting. It is a fact, that Brigham would stop if a buffalo did not fall at the first fire, so as to give me a second chance, but if I did not kill the buffalo then, he would go on, as if to say, 'You are no good, and I will not fool away time by giving you more than two shots.' Brigham was the best horse I ever owned or saw for buffalo chasing."

Cody sold Brigham in 1868 and went into show business, starring on stage and in the outdoor circus of his creation called Buffalo Bill's Wild West. Cody's Wild West extravaganza toured America and Europe for thirty years.

Ever the entrepreneur, he later founded the town of Cody, Wyoming.

Elijah

And the ravens brought him bread and meat in the morning, and bread and meat in the evening; and he drank from the brook.

I KINGS 17:6   THE HOLY BIBLE

Elijah loved his mountains so much he couldn't get back fast enough.

He was a foal of the Rocky Mountains, wild and free, following his mother, his herd, and the four seasons for food, shelter, and fun. His freedom ended when wranglers with heavy ropes and cruel hearts roped him and threw him into a trailer for a trip to a horse seller.

A mountain horse. Surefooted. Smart in the ways of survival. Bill Turner bought Elijah to pack gear for hunters and fishermen into the high country for his and his brother Al's pack-trip company in Buena Vista, Colorado. In the fall of 1955, after one hunt with lots of meat to pack and no room in the trailer, the little brown horse — now called Bugs — was turned loose with another Turner horse named Pinhead to go home.

It is the nature of horses to return to their barn as fast as their legs can carry them. Not Bugs. He turned toward the mountain summit instead, with Pinhead at heel, and snow trapped the two wayward packhorses above timberline.

Providence smiled when a pilot flying overhead happened to spot them on a ridge between Mount Harvard and Mount Yale. A call of alarm went out...they will starve! Haylifts funded by donations were arranged. But when the first half-bale was dropped, only Bugs was seen.

The Denver Post carried Bugs' story. A *Post* editor christened him Elijah, after the Old Testament prophet who was fed by ravens in the wilderness.

Children sent allowance money for hay; offers of homes were proffered; newspapers around the world told the tale. A commercial pilot flew his airliner over the ridge to give his passengers a bird's-eye view of the famous horse.

The Denver Post's team (including a future *National Geographic* photographer) raced the teams of KBTV and KGMC Radio to rescue Elijah. Readers cheered each story.

- "Children Promise Home for Elijah"
- "Haylift Goes on as New Snow Covers Elijah's Lofty Perch"
- "Haylift Is Only Comfort for Marooned Horse"
- "Post Climbers Find Elijah's Fat and Sassy"

The *Post* team reached him first, escorted by the Turner brothers and Buena Vista outdoorswoman Jody Grieb (who went on the fourteen-mile round-trip "just for the walk"). They found Elijah on his mountaintop, fed him, checked him over. After sharing pleasantries, Elijah turned tail and galloped to the back of his hermitage. He wanted to stay.

Bill Turner suggested leaving him until spring thaw when "he'll work his way down all right..."

The public would have none of that! The Turners went after Elijah twice in May. Finally, they dug a trench and started down with Elijah in tow. They couldn't get down in one day, so they stopped and staked out Elijah for the night. But he wriggled free and was headed back up the mountain when, the next morning, the Turners caught him. Again.

Fame was a new experience for Elijah. He was special guest in parades, at parties, and at Denver's posh Brown Palace Hotel. He raced a stable pony named Goliath at Centennial Race Track and won. Then he went back to work packing for hunters and fishermen.

After many years, Elijah was back in his mountains, where he lived out his life, free and wild forevermore.

Elijah, the King of the Rockies

ead high, Elijah stands proud and content on his lofty visit by members of The Denver Post rescue mission, who e straddling the Continental Divide during a Thursday found the snow-trapped horse in prime condition.

Elijah on his mountaintop made page one news in *The Denver Post*.

Mideast Truce Effort Gaining

THE VOICE OF THE ROCKY MOUNTAIN EMPIRE

VOL. 64, NO. 255

Entered as second class matter at postoffice at Denver, Colo., under Act of March 3, 1879.

THE DENVER POST

HOME EDITION
★★★

5 CENTS

60 PAGES

Climate Capital of the World

DENVER, COLORADO, FRIDAY, APRIL 13, 1956

Post Climbers Find Elijah's Fat and Sassy

By GEORGE McWILLIAMS
Denver Post Staff Writer

Elijah the horse roamed a ridge high in the Colorado mountains Friday, fat and sassy after a visit from his owner and a Denver Post snowshoe team.

The rescue party of four men and a woman reached the famous horse at 4:45 p. m. Thursday after a long, hard climb through timber and deep snow to the 12,800-foot ridge between Mt. Harvard and Mt. Yale and 12 air miles west of Buena Vista.

No effort was made to bring Elijah from the lofty saddle he has made his home most of the winter. But the rescue team did answer two questions which have been asked since the horse's plight was discovered seven weeks ago.

One is that Elijah is in better condition than many horses which have wintered in pastures at lower elevation.

The second is that Elijah is definitely Bugs, a packhorse owned by Bill Turner, Buena Vista wrangler who with his brother, Al, operates a packtrain for hunters and fishermen. The Turners, who led the trip Thurs-

Full Page of Photos On Page 26—More Details on Page 2

day to Elijah's ridge, called the horse to them, put a rope halter on him and fed him a box of oats.

Seven members of The Post team drove in a pickup truck to the Collegiate Peaks campground on Middle Cottonwood creek, eight miles west of Buena Vista, and started the climb from there. Two waited on the crest of the first ridge at timberline, while the other five finished the climb to the ridge where Elijah was waiting.

Nothing had been heard Friday morning from a KBTV team of three men which started for Elijah at dawn Thursday, and it was certain they did not reach the final ridge. A plane flying over North Cottonwood creek Friday morning reported a message stamped in the snow near a cabin 1,500 feet below the ridge. It read "KBTV- drop note."

HIS BRAND ON HORSE

Bill Turner said he not only recognized Elijah as his horse Bugs, but found his brand—Heart-Two Bar—on the horse's left shoulder. The Turners said they will try to bring the horse out some time in May when the deep snow has gone and will put him back to work. The one-horse hay-lift which has sustained Elijah through the winter will be continued.

The rescue party which reached the high ridge was composed of the Turners; Dean Conger, Denver Post photographer; Irvin Moss, Post copy boy, and Jody Grieb, 27-year-old Buena Vista woman and member of the Post

'Tired of Running'

Slayer Writes Post, Gives Up To Police Here

By HARRY GESSING
Denver Post Staff Writer

A 30-year-old fugitive parolee wrote The Denver Post a letter saying he was "tired of running" and then surrendered to Denver police Thursday night to finish serving a 12-year prison sentence for murder in Maryland.

Joseph Daniel Brouillette, father of a baby boy, was jailed here to await transportation back to Upper Marlboro, Md. He was convicted of second-degree murder in 1947 for the slaying of a naval officer's wife at a drunken party at Tall Timbers, Md.

He served about five years in the Maryland penitentiary before being paroled to his parents in New Hampshire, he said, but broke his parole by leaving New Hampshire about four years ago.

KEPT JUMPING

Since then, he said, he has been jumping from place to place—to Massachusetts, New Jersey, Ohio, Illinois, Missouri, and finally to Colorado—working a few weeks, always moving on before his past caught up with him. He left his wife and baby early in March in Kansas City, Mo.

Much of the story was contained in a 12-page letter written to The Post and mailed Thursday night. It was delivered Friday morning.

He surrendered to police at 6:30 p. m. and signed a waiver to return to Maryland. Police were notified Friday morning officers would be sent for him.

He said his wife knew nothing

of his murder conviction and parole.

Brouillette told a Denver Post reporter he "never knew a moment's rest" as a fugitive. He "cringed," he said, every time he saw a policeman.

While in Denver, he worked briefly for a baking company, as a dishwasher and for a wholesale clothing company. He stayed at the YMCA and at a private home.

AN AMOROUS HOUR

He told The Post that an official of the baking company and a Lowry air force base sergeant—to whom he told his story Thursday night—both advised him to surrender.

The crew-cut 6-footer, dressed in jeans and a denim shirt, said Friday he could not remember the name of the woman he apparently killed in Maryland. He admitted striking her after an amorous hour in a summer house at the party but said he was not notified until late the next day she was dead.

At that time he was a sailor at a Maryland naval base. After his conviction, the navy discharged him.

He met his wife, he said, during the early days of his parole in New Hampshire. She traveled with him without knowing the reason for his restlessness, he said.

Brouillette said he hopes to start a "new life" after finishing his term.

(More details, photo on page 20)

The POST—MA. 3-2121

THE WEATHER

'Tis a Privilege to Live in Colorado Friday—Sun rose in Denver at 5:28 a.m.; sun sets at 6:36 p.m.

DENVER TEMPERATURES FOR THE LAST TWENTY-FOUR HOURS

THURSDAY		FRIDAY	
1 P. M...	59	1 A. M...	50
2 P. M...	60	2 A. M...	48
3 P. M...	55	3 A. M...	46
4 P. M...	54	4 A. M...	45
5 P. M...	52	5 A. M...	45
6 P. M...	49	6 A. M...	43

Full Discussion Of Mideast On Editorial Page

The Denver Post editorial page today (Page 16) is given wholly to the Arab-Israeli crisis in the middle east. The editors feel this

UN Team Plan Has Arab OK

CAIRO, April 13.—(INS)—The controlled Egyptian press played down the war news Friday as Dag Hammarskjold reportedly made real progress in his quest to restore peace in the middle east.

The United Nations secretary general conferred again Friday with Egyptian Foreign Minister Mahmoud Fawzy in preparation for his meeting Saturday morning with Premier Gamal Abdel Nasser.

Hammarskjold reportedly has already obtained Nasser's approv-

Dag Turns to Israel

UNITED NATIONS, N. Y., April 13.—(INS)—Dag Hammarskjold called on Israel Friday for assurances it has issued orders to Israeli troops against launching new attacks in the Egyptian-held Gaza strip.

The UN secretary general at the same time stated in a communication to Israeli Premier David Ben-Gurion he does not feel recent Egyptian commando attacks inside Israeli territory cast "doubts on the sincerity" of Egypt's pledge to avoid use of force.

al of the first draft of a five-point plan to prevent an all-out Arab-Israeli war.

Members of the Hammarskjold UN mission, cheered by the personal ceasefire pledges of the Egyptian leader and of Israeli Prime Minister David Ben-Gurion, remained unusually tight-lipped about the negotiations under way in Cairo.

But reliable Egyptian sources said the "working proposals" were drawn up at a 60-hour day and night conference.

The plan is believed to provide:

"NO-MAN'S LAND"

1—Withdrawal of frontier forces beyond immediate firing range, thus creating a demilitarized "no-man's land" along the 600-mile Arab-Israeli border.

2—Limitation of front-line arms to short-range weapons.

3—Reduction in armed strength of both sides along the border.

4—Improving communications for UN observers, possibly by adding helicopters.

5—Seeking "agreement in principle" by both sides for a high-level face-to-face conference.

The Egyptian source emphasized that the proposals were still in "rough draft" form with experts on Nasser's staff and in the Hammarskjold mission hammering out details.

HAMMARSKJOLD HOPEFUL.

These included discussion of whether the troops should be withdrawn 300 meters (326 yards), as Nasser once proposed, or 300 meters (328 yards) as later suggested; what kind of arms should be permitted along the front lines, and how large the immediate border area forces should be.

(All quiet on Egypt frontier. Page 5, column 1.)

GOOD 'TROTTER SEATS AVAILABLE

Algonquin

Algonquin and Archie Roosevelt in Washington, D.C., June 17, 1902

Upstairs, downstairs, where can a calico pony not go? In the Theodore Roosevelt White House of hijinks, evidently there were no restrictions.

Fun filled the White House's hallowed halls during the Roosevelt family's residence (1901 to 1909). Family pets included a menagerie of cats, dogs, horses, a small bear, a lizard, a barn owl...and a special pony named Algonquin.

When ten-year-old Archie Roosevelt was recovering from the measles in an upstairs bedroom, he longed to see Algonquin. Sympathizing with patient and pony, Charles (Algonquin's groom) and Kermit and Quentin (Archie's brothers) hatched a plan: Algonquin should pay a sick-bed visit to Archie. The little company led Algonquin into the White House, along its corridors, and into the elevator. Up they went to cheer up Archie.

The New York Times reported: "When the second floor was reached Charles led the pony to Archie's room and ushered it in. To say that Archie was delighted expresses it mildly, and the pony seemed to enjoy the visit. This is the first time that a horse has ridden in a White House elevator."

Algonquin loved seeing his reflection in the elevator mirror and didn't want to get out.

President Roosevelt called Algonquin "...a calico or pinto, being as knowing and friendly as possible." He was given to Archie by Secretary of the Interior Ethan Allen Hitchcock.

Favory Africa

One of Europe's most exquisite treasures, in danger of being stolen by Germans during World War II, was the Lipizzan stallion Favory Africa.

After Germany seized Austria in 1938, German dictator Adolph Hitler selected Favory Africa at the Spanish Riding School in Vienna as a gift for Japanese Emperor Hirohito. Hitler knew that Hirohito favored white horses for ceremonial parades; this gift, he hoped, would further strengthen Germany's war-time ties to Japan.

But Hitler's plan failed, thanks to the foresight and courage of Colonel Alois Podhajsky, director of the Spanish Riding School. Colonel Podhajsky evacuated the Lipizzan stallions to St. Martins, Austria, in early 1945. There, he thought he might protect them.

On May 7, 1945 (the very day Germany surrendered in France), Colonel Podhajsky rode one of his prized Lipizzan stallions for General George S. Patton, Jr., commander of the U.S. Third Army. Following the performance, he halted his horse in front of the general, removed his hat, and requested American protection of the exiled Spanish Riding School. Strident and brave, he asked for more: the rescue of several Lipiz-

zan stallions and more than 200 Lipizzan mares and foals held in Czechoslovakia. He feared they would be slaughtered for meat by starving foreign troops.

Colonel Podhajsky needn't have worried. Patton was a passionate horseman, foxhunter, and polo player who competed in equestrian events in the 1912 Olympic Games in Stockholm. He promised U.S. Army protection for the school. What Patton didn't tell the colonel was that Army forces had already begun "Operation Cowboy," which rescued about 1,000 horses, including the Lipizzans, Thoroughbreds, Arabians, and other breeds in Czechoslovakia.

In August, Patton tried out Favory Africa for himself, aware that he and the U.S. Army had, quite possibly, saved the Lipizzan breed.

The Spanish Riding School turned 450 years old in 2015 and provides the grand setting in Vienna where Lipizzan stallions perform classical horsemanship (haute école, or "high school") and difficult military maneuvers

General George S. Patton, commander of the U.S. Third Army, rides Favory Africa in Austria in August 1945.

called "airs above the ground."

Colonel Podhajsky considered horsemanship, elegantly executed, an art: "Equestrian art, perhaps more than any other, is closely related to the wisdom of life. Many of the same principles may be applied as a line of conduct to follow. The horse teaches us self-control, constancy, and the ability to understand what goes on in the mind and the feelings of another creature, qualities that are important throughout our lives."

Shirayuki

Japanese Emperor Hirohito reviews his troops riding Shirayuki.

As have many military leaders in history, Japanese Emperor Hirohito wanted to review his troops from the back of a white horse.

Prior to the bombing of Pearl Harbor and America's entry into World War II, Hirohito saw the horse he wanted in California. Owner Dewey H. Burden sold the stallion to the Japanese government and Hirohito renamed him Shirayuki (which means "white snow" in Japanese).

Shirayuki starred in many military ceremonies and, with the emperor in his saddle, was featured on the June 10, 1940, cover of *Life* magazine. He was retired in 1942 and died in 1947 at twenty-seven.

6 Heroes and Heroines

These brave horses — and a "wee" pony —
performed with skill and dedication as they
protected their masters.

Sylph

The First Ride: Sylph and Johnny Fry burst from the Pikes Peak Stables on April 3, 1860, the first Pony Express team to carry mail west to California.

The little bay mare danced in place and fidgeted. Her tail hairs had been plucked by souvenir hunters, and the brass band playing patriotic songs on the street set her nerves on edge.

She waited anxiously inside Pikes Peak Stables, raring to go.

Pony Express rider Johnny Fry stayed close and soothed her, knowing the time was near.

It was Tuesday, April 3, 1860, twilight in St. Joseph, Missouri.

St. Joseph Mayor M. Jeff Thompson spoke to the impatient crowd of 40,000: "Hardly will the cloud of dust which envelopes the galloping pony subside before the puff of steam will be seen on the horizon. Citizens of St. Joseph, I bid you give three cheers for the Pony Express."

Mayor Thompson entered the stables

and placed in the mochila (which means "knapsack" in Spanish) forty-nine letters, five telegrams, and several newspapers. The leather mochila, secured to the saddle, had four pockets — or cantinas — to hold mail. The fully loaded mochila weighed less than twenty pounds. Everything was ready and Johnny swung onto the saddle.

At 7:15 p.m.: A cannon BOOM! Johnny squeezed the sides of the mare Sylph, the stable doors flew wide, and they burst into the sea of well-wishers. Johnny reined Sylph toward the Missouri River.

Sylph — though her name in Latin means "slender, graceful girl" — was tough as a Kansas cowboy's boot. Fast and true, she carried Fry. They crossed the river by ferry and hit the trail for Troy, Kansas. At the Troy "relay station," sixteen miles distant, Fry changed horses and Sylph rested as the first horse to carry mail west for the Pony Express.

The question on everyone's mind: Could mail be transported from St. Joseph to Sacramento, California, and from Sacramento to St. Joseph, in a journey of ten days and 1,966 miles…by horseback?

The Central Overland California and Pikes Peak Express Company gambled that it could.

To succeed, the Pony Express required brave riders and hardy horses. About eighty young men answered the newspaper ad looking for: "Young, skinny, wiry fellows not over eighteen. Must be expert riders, willing to risk death daily."

The horsemen rode at breakneck speeds, eight to ten miles per hour, night and day, through snowstorms, rain, herds of buffalo, in scorching heat, across the Rocky Mountains and roaring rivers. Hostilities between the Plains Indians and white settlers increased the danger.

At "relay stations," about 165 buildings built every ten to fifteen miles, riders leaped off their horses, grabbed their mochilas, and vaulted onto fresh, ready-and-waiting horses — in two minutes or less.

At twenty-five "home stations," built ninety to 120 miles apart, weary riders finished their 100 or so miles in the saddle and handed off their mochilas to rested riders. Near the halfway mark, riders exchanged mochilas and turned around, retracing their routes back to where they started, carrying their precious cargo to its final destination. Precious indeed for every one-half ounce cost about $5 in gold, or about $140 today.

(Because of lighter paper, this fee was later reduced to $1 per half-ounce.)

The grand adventure did not last long, only eighteen months. The death knell sounded for the Pony Express when telegraph wires connected the East and West coasts. Operations ceased on October 24, 1861. Pony riders and their 400 to 500 horses had made 616 deliveries between St. Joseph and Sacramento, covering 650,000 miles, and carrying 34,753 pieces of mail.

The Pony Express proved mail could be carried year-round over a central overland route, cutting in half the time required by stagecoach, and providing reliable service with few casualties. One Pony rider froze to death, one drowned in the Platte River in Nebraska, another died when his horse tripped over an ox at night and fell on him. Others lost their lives staffing relay and home stations. Yet only one mochila was lost. An important Pony Express delivery was the announcement in California that Abraham Lincoln had been elected President of the United States.

Though a financial failure, the Pony Express embodied the can-do daring and courageous spirit of the Old West.

Goliath

oliath's nose twitched. His ears pricked back and forth. He stomped one foot, then another.

He knew, he smelled it, he sensed it. A serious fire was seething down the road.

On a regular-routine Sunday morning, everyone in fire-house Engine Company No. 15 readied for inspection. A final burnish to the station house, saddlery, and horses… Clang!! Alarms sounded for downtown Baltimore's John E. Hurst building.

Firemen leaped into fire coats, helmets, and boots.

Goliath and Eugene Short at Engine Company No. 15 in Baltimore

Horses were harnessed to fire wagons. And Goliath — a Percheron weighing about one ton of muscle, flesh and good sense — waited to be hitched to the Hale Water Tower, a key piece of fire-fighting equipment that sprayed water into high-rise windows and onto rooftops.

High winds whipped twigs, debris, and people along the street. Then the winds whipped the Hurst building fire into the Great Baltimore Fire of 1904.

Eugene Short jumped onto the driver's seat. Goliath held the lead position (on Short's outside right-hand side) in the three-horse team that pulled the five-ton water tower. They stopped in front of the Hurst building and saw the fire, by then an inferno, belch billows of flame and cinders and turn the blue sky to reddish orange. Goliath waited as his teammates were unhitched and moved to safety.

Goliath started to become agitated… suddenly the building exploded and fire surged through the entrance, burning and blistering Goliath, who was positioned by the curb.

"It's coming down!" someone yelled, as Goliath pulled away from the curb. Eugene realized he must move the rig and save the water tower so the fire could be fought. Then they could save themselves. "C'mon, let's go, Goliath. Gid' up!" Three big Percherons usually pulled the water tower. Now the task was left to only one — Goliath.

"Let's go, boy!" The rig wouldn't budge. Another slap of the reins. Goliath pulled and strained, his nostrils flaring as red as the fire roaring above his head. He pulled harder.

With one last Herculean effort, Goliath tugged with all the might he could muster and the rig finally moved, first by inches, then forward to safety. At that instant, the Hurst building collapsed in a heap of red bricks and burning wood. Right where Goliath had stood.

The namesake of a strongman in the Bible — a giant of a man who lost his fight — this Goliath won his fight and saved the water tower, Eugene Short, and himself.

From up and down the Eastern seaboard came 1,231 firefighters and 1,200 National Guardsmen to fight the fire that scorched 140 acres of Baltimore. The fire lasted from 10:23 a.m. Sunday, February 7, to about 5 p.m. Monday, February 8, 1904.

Goliath's injuries left scars that bore testament to his resolve to do his duty that day and stand his ground. Big, gentle Goliath recovered for six months in an equine hospital then fought fires for two more years with Engine Company No. 15. A symbol of courage among Baltimore's bravest, Goliath next easily stepped into a new role as goodwill ambassador, greeting visitors to his home station, enjoying hugs and apples from children, and appearing as a special guest at special events.

One such appearance was in the September 1906 "Homecoming Week" parade, when the city of Baltimore recognized the tragedy of the Great Baltimore Fire of 1904 and honored those who fought it. Goliath led the parade wearing a wreath of flowers around his neck.

Snowman

One moment of any one day can change everything forever. That's what happened to a big gray gelding and the horseman Harry de Leyer.

The plow horse that would become famous as Snowman — and the first horse in history to win back-to-back Professional Horsemen's Association (PHA) and American Horse Shows Association (AHSA) Horse of the Year honors — was squished into a tottering old truck with other horses, all bound for the slaughterhouse, when he met Harry.

It was 1956, a cold February morning when Harry left his horse farm in St. James, New York, and drove to a horse auction in Pennsylvania. He arrived late and the auction was over. The horses that didn't sell — the leftovers — were in that truck, including a gray gelding.

Harry wanted to take a look and asked the truck driver to wait. He peeked between the wooden slats and noticed the gray, who moved toward him when Harry offered his hand, and asked that the gray be unloaded. Harry sensed a quiet intelligence about him, a willingness, and a kind heart. He was told the scars on the horse's chest were caused by hours of pulling an

Harry de Leyer gives Snowman full freedom to clear a big jump.

Amish farmer's plow in Pennsylvania Dutch Country.

The gelding displayed some good physical qualities, and with some extra weight Harry thought he might make a good lesson horse at the Knox School, the prestigious girls' boarding school where Harry was riding instructor.

A soft word from Harry, answered in kind by the gray's soft brown eyes, and a connection of kindred spirits was made. That moment changed both their worlds. Acting on instincts learned from a lifetime of living with horses, Harry paid $80 for him.

Harry knew of fear and courage and the power of taking chances. He grew up in Holland during World War II when Nazi Germany occupied and terrorized his country. More than once, thirteen-year-old Harry drove a horse pulling a cart of food for hungry children past Nazi checkpoints. Who is going to stop a little boy and his horse? No one. As an adult, he and his wife left their Dutch homeland to start a life in America. Yes, he thought he'd take a chance with this big gelding.

The gray's $80 price tag included his delivery to the de Leyers' Hollandia Farms. The whole family greeted the thin and dirty horse, who was covered in falling snow.

"Look, Daddy, he has snow all over him. He looks just like a snowman," observed four-year-old Harriet. And Snowman he was named.

Snowman was curried and combed, bathed and brushed, fed good oats and fresh hay. And loved. But Harry had a wife and three children and thought he should sell Snowman when a neighbor came looking for a good horse.

The problem was Snowy just wouldn't have it. He jumped fences and crossed pastures to return to the people and place he loved. Again and again. Harry suggested a horseman's trick to Snowman's new owner: Tie a rubber tire to his lead rope; that will stop his wandering. The trick was tried. Still, early one morning, Harry looked up and there stood Snowy, staring back at him in the Hollandia stable yard, tethered to the tire with pieces of fence caught in the mess. Snowman had jumped his way home. "He kept coming back," Harry recalls. This time he was home for good.

The de Leyer children delighted in their playmate's return. They crawled all over Snowy, shinnied up his tall legs and tail, swam with him in Long Island Sound, and used him as a diving board. At Knox School, Snowy carried the fearful and the fearless with the greatest care.

When time allowed, Harry began teaching Snowman the basics of jumping. They started with caveletti exercises, ground rails evenly spaced in various configurations.

Trotting and cantering over caveletti rails teach a horse balance, timing, discipline, and build muscles. These Snowman tripped over. On to small vertical jumps. He was lackadaisical. But the taller jumps — these got his attention; they challenged him.

Snowy was learning to maneuver his big body over bigger and more difficult fences — tall fences, wide fences, anything Harry pointed him toward. Meanwhile, Harry was campaigning Sinjon, a horse owned by the father of one of his Knox students, in top-level jumping events. They had done so well that the United States Equestrian Team noticed Sinjon and took him for their team. Now, Harry focused on Snowman.

Snowy and Harry (now known as "The Flying Dutchman") first competed in local shows, then moved on to bigger shows and tougher competition. They held their own competing against fancy Thoroughbreds and famous riders — teams often funded by wealthy patrons.

Harry and Snowy plowed up, up, up through the ranks. And in 1958 they competed against the world's best jumpers under the star-spangled lights of America's grandest show, the National Horse Show in New York City's Madison Square Garden. They won the Open Jumper Stakes, which meant they won the National Horse Show Championship.

Alice Higgins, reporting for *Sports Illustrated*, was there: "As the horse cleared the final fence, De Leyer dropped the reins and threw his arms in the air in the exuberant and traditional hurrah gesture; then, as Snowman galloped placidly over the finish, he grabbed the horse around the neck and kissed him." After the show, Harry turned down $35,000 for Snowman.

That year Snowy and Harry captured the Triple Crown of show jumping: the National Horse Show Championship, the American Horse Shows Association Horse of the Year, and the Professional Horsemen's Association Horse of the Year awards. They repeated these Horse of the Year awards again the next year and made history. Snowman's show schedule began to slow. They competed through 1962 and only occasionally thereafter.

"Snowman never caused any trouble. He always did what I asked him to do. It came time for him to retire."

In 1969, Snowman formally said good-bye in a grand retirement ceremony in "The Garden," the site of their greatest victories. Red roses and a green-and-yellow cooler, embroidered with the words "The Cinderella Horse," honored the former plow horse and his owner, trainer, and the man who saved his life, Harry de Leyer.

When it was said to Harry that Snowman was lucky to have found the de Leyers, Harry countered with "I was lucky to find him!"

Snowman lived out his twenty-six years with Harry, grazing good grass and lazing under a favorite tree, always and forever a beloved member of the de Leyer family.

Babe

A white Arabian mare named Babe and Mamie Francis — billed as Miss Mamie — risked life and limb diving off a fifty-foot tower into a ten-foot-deep tank of water. They performed their act 628 times from 1908 to 1914, headlining at Coney Island (New York), Pittsburgh, and Philadelphia. It was unlikely work for Mamie; she couldn't swim.

On July 11, 1908, in front of a festive Coney Island crowd of 30,000, Babe and Mamie inched to the tower's edge. Babe's skin quivered. Mamie focused. Like a banshee's scream, the shrill whistle of a steam calliope shattered the quiet and Babe's concentration. Babe and Mamie tumbled head over hooves into the tank. Rescuers pulled Mamie out, but Babe thrashed underwater, kicking, fighting against drowning. Men tried to loop a rope around her.

Two minutes passed. Then five. Finally, a lone diver, a hero among horses, plunged into the tank and secured the rope around her body. Men encircling the tank wrenched her out. Two hours later Babe walked out of Coney Island.

The near-death experience daunted neither Babe nor Mamie. They continued to climb that ramp and leap from the platform, trusting their own abilities and each other.

Mamie loved the act: "...and when (Babe) jumps, oh, the glory of it all. I just close my eyes, take a deep breath, and await the splash."

Even so, she admitted she high-dived for money.

"After a while, I will be able to retire and live on my ranch without bothering over money matters. Until then, I must take the chance of accident involved in the high dive on horseback. But...I have minimized the chance...not by any trickery or chicanery, but by skill. Everything depends upon myself and my horse."

Mamie might have leaped for money. But Babe leaped for Miss Mamie.

Babe and Mamie Francis leap from a fifty-foot tower to a shallow pool below. Mamie was inducted into the National Cowgirl Museum's Hall of Fame in 1981.

Olga

Olga is one of only four horses to be awarded the Dickin Medal from England's PDSA (People's Dispensary for Sick Animals).

On July 3, 1944, during World War II German bombing raids on London, Olga was working Besley Street in Tooting in south London. A bomb exploded 300 feet from her, killing four people, destroying four houses, and shattering a plate glass into a million pieces at her feet.

Panicked at first and bolting, she quickly calmed and returned to the scene to help her rider PC J. E. Thwaites with crowd control and first aid.

She and two equine partners on the police force —

Regal and Upstart — were awarded the Dickin Medal in a ceremony at Hyde Park on April 11, 1947. The medal recognized all the nearly 200 horses of London's Metropolitan Police mounted division who served during World War II.

Sergeant Reckless received the award in 2016. And Warrior received an honorary PDSA Dickin Medal in 2014 on behalf of all the animals who served during World War II.

The Dickin Medal is commonly referred to as the Victoria Cross (the highest decoration for service during wartime) for animals and honors Maria Dickin, the founder of PDSA who established the award.

Olga (far left), Regal (middle), and Upstart receive the Dickin Medal in London's Hyde Park for heroism during World War II.

Captain

"I once had a sweet wee pony called Captain." Captain worked hard as a pit pony deep in the Scottish coal mines during the late 1800s. His usual driver was a young Scot, the singing Harry Lauder. One day, with Lauder riding behind in "a little tub" (or "hutch" as they are called in Scotland), Captain halted and about-faced like a goose-stepping soldier on parade. His tiny feet hustled in the opposite direction despite Lauder's protestations.

Seconds later, the pit roof fell.

"Captain's instinct had told him that something was going to happen; his acute ears had heard warning sounds which to mine were quite unintelligible." Then "tons upon tons came down from the roof."

Captain had saved both their lives. "When I realised what had taken place the tears came to my eyes. I threw my arms round wee Captain's neck and kissed and cuddled him again and again."

Lauder left mining for fame as a singer, songwriter, and comedian. King George V knighted him in 1919 for fund-raising to benefit World War I soldiers returning to civilian life. He also campaigned for good homes for retiring pit ponies and good treatment of those still working the mines.

Sir Lauder remembered Captain as a "wise wee boy."

A pit pony toils underground in a Scottish mine, circa 1900-1910.

7 STARS OF THE SHOW

These horses jumped big fences, won in the show ring, and bucked off cowboys in rodeo arenas.

Huaso

Huaso clears the record-setting height of eight feet, one and a quarter inches.

The highest jump by a horse, say Guinness World Records and the Fédération Equestre Internationale, was eight feet, one and a quarter inches (2.47 meters), a record set by the Chilean jumper Huaso.

(He was originally named Faithful; in training his name was changed to Huaso, which is the Chilean word for cowboy or rustic peasant.)

On February 5, 1949, a summer evening in the seaside town of Chile's Viña del Mar, Captain Alberto Larraguibel Morales warmed up seventeen-year-old Huaso, a 16.2-hand, dark bay Thoroughbred. Watching were 5,000 spectators, President of the Republic don Gabriel González

Videla, and military, civilian and equestrian elite — all on the edge of their seats, hoping to see history made. If successful, one of two teams would give Chile its first world record in any sport.

The competition pitted Huaso against another Chilean team, Chileno and Lieutenant Luis Riquelme. Each team had three chances to clear the obstacle. The jump was set at six feet (1.83 meters), which both horses cleared. It was raised to seven feet (2.14 meters). Huaso jumped it cleanly; it took Chileno two tries to clear it.

The riders and judges talked: Let's add two logs and make it 2.47 meters, two centimeters higher than the world record.

Chileno jumped it first, and down toppled a log. The lieutenant guided Chileno again to the towering jump; again, a knockdown. Huaso was up next. Captain Larraguibel Morales analyzed the distance and the best takeoff spot, then pressed Huaso forward. But Huaso didn't like the looks of it and refused.

Now, a second try. The captain asked Huaso again for an enormous effort; Huaso gathered himself, tucked his front legs, and up and over! Yet…his big body rubbed the big jump and a log fell.

Chileno, brave but tiring, faced the jump again. He managed the takeoff, but hit the top logs. He and the lieutenant fell together to the ground, unhurt but disappointed that they had no more chances.

Huaso had one more try. With history at stake, Huaso soared as if with wings and cleared the jump.

Captain Larraguibel Morales recalled the moment: "As I approached the jump I prompted him by slackening the reins with my hands. Huaso peaked just at the spot where I had felt that he should, and, with a magical display of flexibility, power, resolve and grace, he flew through the air."

Huaso and the captain catapulted to national-hero status and are honored today with a monument in Alberto Larraguibel Square in Santiago, the capital of Chile.

"From my end, it was as if I had flung my heart over the obstacle and was now going over it to retrieve it."

Big Ben

Big Ben and Ian Millar in Germany

Big Ben, even though he was born in Belgium, forever remains a favorite son of Canada.

He arrived in Canada in 1983 with the name Winston and began training with Canadian rider Ian Millar. Towering in talent and height — he stood 17.3 hands — the Belgian Warmblood got a new name and he and Millar set out to set records.

The Big Ben–Millar team finished in the top eight in five consecutive World Cup competitions and was the first team to win back-to-back World Cup finals (1988 and 1989). They competed in three Olympic Games. In the 1987 Pan American Games in Indianapolis, Indiana, Millar rode Big Ben to two gold medals, one in individual competition and another in team competition as members of the Canadian Equestrian Team.

They represented Canada on seven winning Nations Cup teams and twice won the du Maurier Ltd. International Grand Prix (which boasted the richest Grand Prix prize money in the world at the time) at Calgary's Spruce Meadows.

After their second du Maurier victory in 1991, before a crowd of 28,000, Millar gave the big chestnut his due.

"I want to make sure everyone knows who the true champion is," said Millar. "It's this magnificent horse. He's one of the best show jumpers that ever lived. I can't tell you how lucky and blessed I feel to have been able to escort this horse around courses."

Big Ben was the first North American show jumper to win more than $1.5 million, collecting more than fifty Grand Prix championships along the way. They were the first team to capture a World Cup by winning all three segments of competition.

Big Ben's show-jumping career ended in 1994. But before sweet retirement at Millar Brooke Farm in Perth, Ontario, Big Ben toured Canada to bid good-bye to his legions of fans. The big gelding died in 1999 at age twenty-three.

"Ben won everything — World Cup finals indoors, derbies in big fields outdoors, on grass, sand, mud, in wind, sunshine, rain, hail, against all odds, and when he was the clear favourite, Big Ben did not disappoint,"

praised Millar.

Big Ben is remembered in many ways. *For the Love of a Horse*, a bronze statue of him and Millar clearing a big triple oxer, graces Big Ben Park in downtown Perth. They were inducted into Canada's Sports Hall of Fame in 1996 and honored with a Canadian postage stamp in 1999. Breyer featured Big Ben in its line of model horses.

Everyone loved Big Ben. Especially Ian Millar.

Flanagan

P at Smythe was the first woman to win an Olympic medal in show jumping, a feat accomplished riding the big chestnut Flanagan.

Competing for the British Equestrian Team, she rode Flanagan in the 1956 Olympic Games in Stockholm, Sweden, when the British team won the bronze medal behind Germany and Italy.

She praised Flanagan's courage: "His brave heart that carried him through the supreme test of guts, and his preparation for the ordeal, place him at once in the select company of the bravest and best horses from other nations."

The pair competed in the Olympics again four years later in Rome, and Flanagan helped her win the European Ladies Championship four times.

"Flanagan, with his easy temperament and buoyant school-boy spirit, had always had a go at every fence that came in his way."

A water jump challenges Flanagan and Pat Smythe during the Olympic trials in Windsor (England), March 28, 1956.

King Tut

King Tut and Bonnie Gray Harris jump a car on her wedding day, with her groom and bridesmaid in the back seat.

Wedding day bells could have turned into wedding day blues in 1930 for Bonnie Gray Harris. But King Tut carried the day when he jumped a four-door touring car with Bonnie on his back and her groom and bridesmaid tucked (ever-so-tightly) in the backseat.

Reba Perry Blakely saw the daring pair perfectly perform the stunt in 1927 and wrote: "Bonnie sat right up there in the middle of King Tut, giving him full freedom of his jumping powers to just take off, go high into the air like an exploding shower of Fourth of July fire bombs and land with King Tut's momentum intact as that gallant huge Palomino almost nodded his head to the audience's applause.

"You could tell by his strut after leaping over the car and the way he pinpricked his ears forward he was as pleased as punch he hadn't misjudged his leap, hadn't put a foot into a passenger's mouth or bashed their hats in… or heads!"

Bonnie, aka the "King Tut Cowgirl," was a famous trick rider, professional rodeo rider, and movie stuntwoman. She was inducted into the National Cowgirl Museum's Hall of Fame in 1981 and died in 1988 at ninety-six years old.

Rugged Lark

Carol Harris and her beloved champion Rugged Lark

In the world of American Quarter Horses, winning the Superhorse title is tantamount to being crowned a versatile king or queen. This special horse earns the honor by earning the most points in three or more events in at least two categories during the American Quarter Horse Asssociation's (AQHA) World Championship Show in Oklahoma City.

It isn't easy.

Rugged Lark tried twice and won twice — in 1985 when he was four and in 1987 when he was six. He was the first Superhorse to sire a Superhorse. In fact, he sired *two* Superhorses — The Lark Ascending, who won in 1991, and Look Whos Larkin, winning in 1999. Another son, Regal Lark, missed the Superhorse title by only one point in 1993 and earned the reserve title.

A stunning bay stallion, Rugged Lark was foaled in 1981 at Bo-Bett Farm in Reddick, Florida. His sire was the well-bred Thoroughbred Really Rugged by Ruff N Tumble; he was out of the AQHA Champion mare Alisa Lark, by Leolark.

Lark reveled under the tutelage of fine trainers: Bo-Bett's resident trainer Mike Corrington began his early education. Lynn Palm introduced him to driving, dressage, western pleasure, western riding, trail, and bridleless riding. Barbara Williams and Bob Loomis honed his reining talents, and Colleen McQuay helped Lynn introduce him to hunters over fences and on the flat.

He transitioned easily from western to English disciplines, always willing to try and succeeding at everything. He won his second Superhorse title competing in hunter under saddle, reining, western riding, working hunter, pleasure driving, hunter hack, and trail.

In 1987, as Lynn rode Rugged Lark into the arena for the Superhorse award ceremony, his owner and breeder Carol Harris surprised the crowd with an announcement: Rugged Lark was retiring from the show ring. "He'd earned the right to go home to Florida and stay with his mares."

Carol recalls the moment. "The crowd's applause was deafening as they stood and watched Lark's victory gallop turn into a bridleless, lead-changing performance.

His fans realized they were watching exactly what an American Quarter Horse was meant to be."

She oversaw his care and career like a British royal's nanny.

"He was so sensitive and intelligent, I was determined that he was never subjected to any kind of intimidation or abuse. I made absolutely sure that he would always be cued with a gentle light hand and a soft voice, when he was led, groomed, introduced to visitors, or supervised at parties to which he was continually invited!"

She felt that though Lark was a breeding stallion, "if he was handled carefully and correctly, he would continue to respect everyone and could be totally trusted…even without a halter or bridle."

Lark boasted brains, athleticism, and show business savvy.

"We loved him dearly only to have him always repay us by being the best he could be. His popularity was like living with Elvis," Carol said, "but best of all

he was a healthy, happy horse who for twenty-three years required the services of a veterinarian only two times in his entire life." Once was at the American Quarter Horse Congress when he was treated for hives; the second was for colic, which ended his life in 2004.

While exhibiting across America, he won AQHA's Silver Spur Award (for his gift of entertainment); was featured as a best-selling Breyer horse; and was profiled in the book *America's Super Horse, The Story of Rugged Lark* (by Rebekah Ferran Witter) and the DVD *Rugged Lark, His Final Days.*

In 2006, Rugged Lark was inducted into the American Quarter Horse Hall of Fame in Amarillo, Texas. Greeting visitors to the American Quarter Horse Hall of Fame & Museum is a bronze sculpture of Lark and Carol called *Ambassadors,* sculpted by Marrita McMillian.

Rugged Lark was lovingly laid to rest between two orange trees on Bo-Bett Farm.

Snowbound

Snowbound and William C. Steinkraus in Europe

Snowbound made history when he carried William C. Steinkraus to the first individual gold medal ever won by an American rider. Their victory came during the 1968 Summer Olympics in Mexico City.

Foaled in 1958 in California, Snowbound started life with the name Gay Vic and a future on the Thoroughbred racetrack. Neither name nor profession fit him. One day in 1962, his discouraged train-

er left him in an empty stall in the home stable of future Show Jumping Hall of Famer Barbara Worth Oakford. She had been away at a horse show and found four-year-old Gay Vic, with his two bowed tendons, when she returned. "With all his faults, he might as well be snowbound as to think of being a show horse!" she exclaimed.

Luckily, a new career bloomed for the newly named Snowbound when he showed a talent for show jumping. After a brief and promising start as a show hunter, he was sold as a jumper prospect and loaned to the United States Equestrian Team. From 1965 to 1968, he won many top level international competitions, including the Grands Prix of New York, London, and Harrisburg, and proved to be a solid anchor on America's Nations Cup teams, contributing to Nations Cup victories in Harrisburg, London, Dublin, and all over Europe.

In Mexico City, he proved superior among forty-two horses of the world's best in two rounds of jumping and over a course that featured one monstrous jump after another, including a six-foot wall and an oxer that got everyone's attention: Parallel bars with rails set at five feet, nine inches; and six feet with a spread of more than seven feet. Snowbound's one knockdown came here. They cleared the rest of the course to win the gold medal.

Steinkraus wrote in 2009: "We never tried to see how big a fence (Snowbound) actually could jump...But within the range of his scope, he was just an exceptionally clean and versatile jumper, and as game as horses come. You felt you could ride him through the eye of a needle and that if you pointed him at a house, he'd try to jump it.

"Nothing ever fazed him; indeed, I can't recall that he ever stopped at a fence in his entire career, and you could count the faults he had over water on one hand."

Snowbound enjoyed a happy retirement in Ireland and was inducted into the Show Jumping Hall of Fame in 2004. Steinkraus was inducted in 1987.

Steamboat

Steamboat was born in Laramie, Wyoming, around the turn of the twentieth century and could be counted on (for he was a professional) to always buck. He knew his job. In fourteen years on the rodeo circuit, he never failed to give it his all.

Cowboys riding him knew they had work at hand when they heard him whistle through his nose — like a steamboat. That's how he got his name. At a rodeo in Cheyenne in 1905, bronc rider Otto Plaga rode Steamboat for eighty-eight jumps before being ejected.

Steamboat died about 1915. He is honored with a plaque in the Memorial Gardens of the National Cowboy & Western Heritage Museum in Oklahoma City and was inducted into the ProRodeo Hall of Fame in 1979.

Many westerners have long believed that Steamboat was the model for Wyoming's iconic "Bucking Horse and Rider" vehicle license plates.

Wyoming Secretary of State Lester C. Hunt designed the plate in 1936, using only cowboy "Stub" Farlow in mind. No mention of a horse.

Guy Holt tries to stay aboard Steamboat in a Laramie (Wyoming) rodeo, 1903.

King's Pistol

King's Pistol and Jim Calhoun work a calf in 1961. This photograph was used to create an early logo of the National Cutting Horse Association.

K ing's Pistol was a treasure beyond measure. During the early years of the National Cutting Horse Association (NCHA), he emerged to set a benchmark of excellence. To his human family, Pistol was worth more than a you-fill-in-the-

amount blank check.

Jim Calhoun of Cresson, Texas, bought the "short-legged, pot-bellied" two-year-old colt in 1952 in Oklahoma, thinking he'd make a good working ranch horse. The little bay's pedigree impressed him: a son of King P-234 and Flit,

daughter of the famous Quarter Horse Leo. (Flit set a track record while carrying him.)

Pistol also sparked interest in H. Calhoun, Jim's father and an NCHA founder. He suggested that Jim give Pistol a chance — see how he works out under saddle

(Continued on next page)

King's Pistol (continued)

then, maybe, as a sire. That was good advice, as it turned out.

Early on Pistol revealed his intelligence and cow sense. Sometimes riding on their ranch, Jim and Pistol practiced cutting a calf from the herd. When a calf got away, Pistol would have to kick into high gear to move the calf back to the fence.

At their next cutting event, Jim "drove a yearling out of the bunch and the old horse just held her up against the arena fence and wouldn't let her go anywhere. I couldn't keep him off the fence without taking hold of him. He'd jump out there and head the cow before she ever got started.

"If a horse is smart, he'll figure out how to get the job done with the least amount of effort," Jim said.

Pistol began showing and by age four had earned American Quarter Horse Association (AQHA) points in halter, reining, and cutting, and was named an AQHA champion. In 1957, he was Open Superior Cutting Champion, Open NCHA World Champion, and earned his Performance Register of Merit (ROM).

Early in 1958, Pistol won halter honors, the cutting class, and the NCHA Open Cutting class at a Quarter Horse show in Odessa, Texas. Jim decided that after Odessa, he would show Pistol just once more — at the big Fort Worth Fat Stock Show. After winning the NCHA Open Cutting championship and $21,821.33 in NCHA cuttings, Pistol went home to pass on more of those good bloodlines.

Pistol's first-generation offspring of 236 foals were multi-talented, multitaskers. There were cutting horses, reiners, halter champions, and one good racehorse. One of his finest was the 1954 mare King's Michelle. She was the 1960 Open Superior Cutting champion, the AQHA 1962 Open High Point Cutting Mare champion, reserve champion in the 1962 Open NCHA World Champion standings, and won $31,604 in NCHA events.

Pistol's gray daughter Pistol Lady 2 Be produced House Mouse and Miss Silver Pistol, two mares who together won more than $1.2 million in NCHA events. Then there were the dun daughter King's Pistola, an AQHA champion with Superior Halter and Performance ROM honors; the fast racehorse Pistol Mike; and the outstanding reiner Pistol's Machete, among many others.

Pistol was superlative at all he attempted. Once Jim received a letter containing a signed, blank check, and a note asking to buy Pistol. Name your own price. Jim returned it. You can't sell family.

Pistol died at home in 1969 at nineteen years old.

8 Legend and Lore

These four horses, though ancient and myth-ological in origin, are seen and heard today in art, advertising, and language.

Pegasus

Pegasus was a brilliant flying horse, tended by the nine Muses.

A flying horse comes in handy when killing a fire-breathing beast tops this week's to-do list.

That was Bellerophon's mission: kill the Chimaera, one of Greek mythology's scariest characters. She was making life miserable for the kingdom of Lycia. Many warriors tried to kill her, and all failed.

But Bellerophon was different. He was young, handsome, a fine horseman, and soldier without peer. More than anything else, he wanted Pegasus, the flying horse, as his own. He longed for him and dreamed of riding him through the clouds. So desperate was he for Pegasus that he consulted the soothsayer Polyidus.

Polyidus told him to spend a night in the temple of Athena, the goddess of war and wisdom. Perhaps she could help.

Bellerophon followed the soothsayer's advice and fell into a deep sleep. He dreamed he saw Athena and heard her speak. "Asleep? Nay, wake. Here is what will charm the steed you covet." He awoke and found at his feet the golden bridle that would tame Pegasus.

Pegasus was the grandest of all horses, brave, beautiful, tended by the nine Muses. He flew over the mountains, earth and sea, wild and free; his snowy-white feathered wings cleaved the air with power and grace. When he landed to drink from the spring Pirene, Bellerophon slipped on the bridle.

All was well until Bellerophon visited King

Proetus in the city of Argos. He so charmed Proetus's wife that she fell in love with him. The king, mad with jealousy, asked Bellerophon to deliver a letter to Iobates, king of Lycia. The king opened the letter: "Kill Bellerophon!" it said.

That request presented a problem. Zeus, the chief Greek god, insisted that hosts honor their guests. And no one dared cross Zeus. Iobates hatched an idea: *Why not send Bellerophon to kill the Chimaera? He will probably die trying to kill the Chimaera. Then I solve two problems.*

Bellerophon agreed to the task and vaulted onto Pegasus's back, tucked between his wings, and off they soared. Bellerophon had two weapons other warriors lacked: mighty Pegasus and a ball of lead mounted on the tip of his spear.

They found the Chimaera spitting fire and belching smoke. She was a lion in front, a goat in the middle, and behind — the tail of a serpent that writhed back and forth angrily. Pegasus circled, moved closer, then hovered. When her head drew back and roared, her mouth gaping wide and open, Bellerophon aimed and fired. The ball hurtled down her throat, was set afire by her breath, and incinerated her insides. She was dead.

Bellerophon's triumph over the Chimaera and in other trials impressed Iobates. He gave Bellerophon his daughter to marry and his kingdom to rule. But Bellerophon grew proud and fancied himself equal to the immortals who lived on Mount Olympus.

One day Bellerophon rode Pegasus above the clouds to the gates of Mount Olympus, thinking he should live there, too. What folly! Zeus sent a gadfly to sting Pegasus, who then bucked Bellerophon off. He tumbled head over heels to earth and roamed homeless forevermore, proving that pride comes before a fall.

And what of Pegasus? He lived in Zeus's royal stables and carried his lightning bolts and thunder.

The Trojan Horse

Have you ever received a gaily wrapped gift, beribboned and begging to be opened? You tear it open and — surprise! — it's a box of rocks. That's what happened to the people of Troy.

The Trojans had been at war with the Greeks for ten long years. The feud started when Paris of Troy stole the wife of Menelaus, the king of Sparta. Her name was Helen and she was the most beautiful woman in the world. Paris wanted her for himself. When he arrived at Menelaus' palace, Eros (you may know him as Cupid) shot Helen with an arrow of love and she fell instantly in love with Paris.

Helen and Paris eloped and the Greeks went after her, camping on the shore of Troy. Many great Greek

The Trojan Horse held a surprise for the people of Troy.

and Trojan warriors died over the next decade.

With everyone weary and neither side winning, the clever Greek soldier Odysseus hatched an idea. The Greek army built a huge wooden horse and left it on the beach, then sailed away, (presumably) in defeat.

The high priest Laocoon cautioned the Trojans. "Trust not their presents, nor admit the horse."

But the people of Troy didn't listen. They opened wide the city gates and pulled the wooden horse into the heart of Troy, their trophy (they thought) for their great victory over the Greeks. All of Troy celebrated and feasted into the night.

When the city fell quiet and the full moon rose, the horse's hollow belly opened and out poured Greek soldiers. They had not left at all; they had only hidden behind a nearby island to make it appear so. The Trojans were killed, captured, or ran away; the city was destroyed; and Helen of Troy returned to Menelaus.

From The Trojan Horse tale comes the proverbial expression: "Beware of Greeks bearing gifts."

Sleipnir

Sleipnir was a brave eight-legged horse from Norse mythology.

If all horses had eight legs, they too might soar over land and sea, enter the underworld, and safely return. Only Sleipnir, the great gray stallion from Norse mythology, could boast such gifts. The swiftest and strongest of all steeds, Sleipnir was owned by Odin, ruler of the heavenly city of Asgard.

Another special member of Odin's household was Balder. Balder the Beautiful, he was called, the much-loved god of light, the son of Odin and Frigga.

But the trickster god, Loki, was jealous of Balder. Like Achilles and his heel, Balder had one vulnerability: He could be slain only by the piercing of a mistletoe branch. Loki guided the aim of a shooter, the mistletoe found its mark, and Balder died.

All of Asgard grieved as Balder entered the dark, cold land ruled by Hel, the goddess of death. Overcome with their loss, Odin and Frigga devised a possible escape for Balder, but they would have to rely on the compassion of Hel; the courage of another son, Hermod; and the mighty Sleipnir.

Sleipnir and Hermod set out to the land of Hel, down, down, cold and colder, for nine days and nine nights. Sleipnir gallantly galloped across the gold-and-crystal bridge (which hung by one hair) that spanned the icy river Gjöll; past the snarling guard dog Garm; and up to the iron Hel-gate. When Hermod asked, Sleipnir jumped the gate and delivered him to Hel.

"Please let Balder return to Asgard," Hermod begged. "Without him, Asgard can never again be happy!" Hel said she'd release Balder if everyone and everything in Asgard wept for him.

All did, except Loki, who refused to weep Balder out of the underworld. Hermod's rescue failed; Sleipnir's courage and eight legs got him to the land of Hel (and back to Asgard) to try.

> *And he will fare across the dismal ice*
> *Northward, until he meets a stretching wall*
> *Barring his way, and in the wall a grate.*
> *But then he must dismount, and on the ice*
> *Tighten the girths of Sleipnir, Odin's horse,*
> *And make him leap the grate, and come within.*
>
> — An excerpt from "Balder Dead," by Matthew Arnold

Lady Godiva's Horse

Lady Godiva hoped to lower taxes for the townspeople of Coventry.

Lady Godiva rode into history by way of a bet.

She was a British noble-man's wife, a lady of means and modesty, and friend to the common folk. Godiva begged her husband, Leofric, the earl of Mer-cia, to reduce taxes on the people of Coventry, England.

To stop her whining (and for fun), he promised to lower taxes if she'd ride naked through town. So the compassionate equestrienne — who lived circa 1040 to 1080 — paraded through Coventry's busy marketplace wearing no clothes.

Legend says she asked the good people of Coventry to show their support by shuttering their windows as she rode past. But a tailor named Tom peeked and the "Peeping Tom" has been with us since.

The earl removed all taxes, except those on horses. Her horse probably didn't care, but he might have liked his name to be known, which it isn't.

Photo Credits

Cover: Napoleon Crossing the Grand Saint-Bernard Pass, 20 May 1800, 1802 (oil on canvas), David, Jacques Louis (1748 – 1825)/ Château de Versailles, France/Bridgeman Images.

Chapter 1

1. Eohippus. Photo by Gayle Stewart, courtesy of the Kentucky Horse Park, Lexington, Kentucky.
2. The Byerley Turk. Reproduced courtesy of Fores Gallery and Thomas Ross Limited. Goldsborough Hall, North Yorkshire, England, courtesy of Mark Oglesby.
3. The Darley Arabian. Reproduced courtesy of Fores Gallery and Thomas Ross Limited.
4. The Godolphin Arabian. ©Bettmann/CORBIS.
5. Blaze. Photo of Prince Cedric III, courtesy of the Clydesdale Breeders of the U.S.A., Pecatonica, Illinois.
6. Eclipse. George Stubbs (English, 1724 1806), Eclipse with Mr. Wildman and His Sons, 1769 1771, oil on canvas, 40 x 50 in. (101.6 x 127.1 cm), The Baltimore Museum of Art, William Woodward Collection, BMA 1956.282.
7. Pluto. Morning Exercise in the Hofreitschule, Josephsplatz. Blaas, Julius von. (b. 1845 – 1923). Kunsthistorisches Museum, Vienna, Austria/Bridgeman Images.
8. Justin Morgan. Courtesy of the American Morgan Horse Association, Shelburne, Vermont.
9. Gaines' Denmark 61. Charcoal drawing by George Ford Morris. Courtesy of the American Saddlebred Museum, Lexington, Kentucky.
10. Wimpy P-1. Courtesy of the King Ranch©, Kingsville, Texas.
11. Hambletonian 10. Courtesy of the U.S. Trotting Association, Columbus, Ohio.
12. Creation's King. Courtesy of the American Hackney Horse Society, Lexington, Kentucky.
13. Dawndee. Courtesy of the Appaloosa Horse Club, Moscow, Idaho.
14. Old Billy, a Draught Horse, Aged 62. Charles Towne, Manchester Museum, The University of Manchester.

Chapter 2

15. Occident. Iris & B. Gerald Cantor Center for Visual Arts at Stanford University; Stanford Family Collections, JLS.13928.
16. "Tennessee Stud." Don Warden Music Co., Brentwood, Tennessee.
17. Rocinante. ClipArt ETC.
18. Lady Suffolk. Currier and Ives. Public domain.
19. Trigger. Photofest.
20. Buttermilk. Courtesy of David Rothel, *The Roy Rogers Book* author.
21. Silver. American Broadcasting Co./Photofest.
22. Daredevil. Disney/Photofest.
23. Gunpowder. Disney/Photofest.
24. Samson. Disney/Photofest.
25. The Piebald. Metro-Goldwyn-Mayer/Photofest.
26. Gulliver and the Houyhnhnms. Drawing by J. J. Grandville (1803 – 1847). Public domain.
27. Misty of Chincoteague, sculpted by Brian Maughan, courtesy of Holt Shotwell and the Chincoteague Chamber of Commerce (Virginia).
28. Black Beauty. Dover Digital Design Source.
29. Merrylegs. ©Warner Bros./Photofest.
30. Mr. Butler. Selznick International Pictures/Photofest.
31. The Black Stallion. Zoetrope Studios/Photofest.
32. Mister Ed. Metro-Goldwyn-Mayer/Photofest.
33. Flicka. 20th Century Fox/Photofest.
34. Champion. ©Autry Qualified Interest Trust and The Autry Foundation.
35. The Maltese Cat. Illustration from "The Maltese Cat," from Animal Stories by Rudyard Kipling, published in 1932 (colour litho), Tresilian, Stuart (1891 – 1976)/Private Collection/Bridgeman Images.

Chapter 3

36. Joey. DreamWorks/Photofest.
37. Midnight Ride of Paul Revere. From a calendar, circa 1930s. GraphicaArtis/Corbis.
38. Traveller. Photo by Michael Miley. Lee Chapel Collections, Washington and Lee University, Lexington, Virginia.
39. Cincinnati. National Archives, Mathew Brady Collection.
40. Little Sorrel. From the original painting by Mort Künstler, Stonewall Jackson on Little Sorrel, ©2001 Mort Künstler, Inc., www.mkunstler.com.
41. Winchester. Military History. Smithsonian Institution.
42. Black Jack. Courtesy of the Canadian County (Oklahoma) Historical Museum, El Reno, Oklahoma. Donated by Lottie Jones. And AP.
43. Old Bob. Abraham Lincoln Presidential Library & Museum (ALPLM), Springfield, Illinois.
44. Alexander and Bucephalus, sculpted by John Steell (1804 - 91), stands in the quadrangle of Edinburgh City Chambers, Scotland. Lloyd Smith, photographer. Courtesy of Edinburgh City Archives.
45. Reckless. National Archives.
46. Comanche. The Kansas State Historical Society, Topeka, Kansas.
47. Vic. Courtesy of Jed Clauss, Amereon Ltd.
48. Battle of Marengo, (engraving), French School, (19th century)/Private Collection/@Look and Learn/Elgar Collection/Bridgeman Images.
49. Copenhagen. The Duke of Wellington, KG LVO OBE MC DL: Photograph courtesy of the Courtauld Institute of Art, London.
50. Siete Leguas. Courtesy of the El Paso Public Library, El Paso, Texas.

Chapter 4

51. Man o' War. George S. Bolster Collection of the Saratoga Springs History Museum, Saratoga Springs, New York.
52. Secretariat. Bob Coglianese photo.
53. Aristides. Art by Beverley Bryant, from her book Portraits In Roses.
54. Survivor. ClipArt ETC., S. G. Goodrich. The Animal Kingdom Illustrated. (New York: A. J. Johnson & Co., 1885). 588. Courtesy, the private collection of Roy Winkelman.
55. Ruthless. Courtesy of the Keeneland Library, Lexington, Kentucky.
56. Sir Barton. Courtesy of the Canadian Horse Racing Hall of Fame.
57. Red Rum. Colorsport/Andrew Cowie.
58. Phar Lap. Courtesy of Racetrack Magazine, Sydney, Australia.
59. Jay Trump. Courtesy of the Winants family and the Maryland Thoroughbred Breeders Association.
60. Battleship. ©Bettmann/CORBIS.
61. Citation. Keeneland-Cook photo.
62. Seabiscuit. Courtesy of the Seabiscuit Heritage Foundation.
63. Seattle Slew. The Blood-Horse/Anne M. Eberhardt
64. Affirmed. The Blood-Horse/Anne M. Eberhardt
65. Smuggler. Courtesy of Jeffrey Tillou Antiques, Litchfield, Connecticut.
66. Dan Patch. Minnesota Historical Society.
67. 1957 Kentucky Derby. The Blood-Horse
68. Special Effort. Courtesy of Ruidoso Downs Race Track, Ruidoso, New Mexico.
69. American Pharoah. Courtesy of Blood-Horse LLC/Anne M. Eberhardt.
70. Black Gold. Churchill Downs, Inc./Kinetic Corporation.
71. Cannonade. ©The Courier-Journal, Louisville, Kentucky.
72. Devon Loch. AP Photo.
73. Justify. Courtesy of Blood-Horse LLC/Anne M. Eberhardt.

Chapter 5

74. Manitou. Theodore Roosevelt Collection, Houghton Library, Harvard University.
75. Teddy. Photo courtesy of Will Rogers Memorial Museums, Claremore, Oklahoma.
76. Macaroni. Robert Knudsen. White House Photographs. John F. Kennedy Presidential Library and Museum, Boston, Massachusetts.
77. Burmese. Photo by Diane Fisher, courtesy of Fred Rasmussen, Tofield, Alberta, Canada.
78. Brigham. Photograph by Carolyn Seelen, courtesy of National Cowboy & Western Heritage Museum, Oklahoma City. Leonard McMurry sculpture.
79. Elijah. Story by George McWilliams, photograph by Dean Conger. The Denver Post, April 13, 1956, page one.
80. Algonquin. Photograph by Frances Benjamin Johnston. Library of Congress Prints and Photographs Division, Washington, D.C.
81. Favory Africa. National Archives. Photo #208-PU-154G-5.
82. Shirayuki. National Archives. Photo #208-PU-935-4.

Chapter 6

83. Sylph. Oil painting by Charles Hargens. Courtesy of the Pony Express National Museum, St. Joseph, Missouri.
84. Goliath. Courtesy of the Fire Museum of Maryland, Lutherville, Maryland.
85. Snowman. George Silk/LIFE Picture Collection/Getty Images.
86. Babe. National Cowgirl Museum and Hall of Fame, Fort Worth, Texas.
87. Olga. Courtesy of The People's Dispensary for Sick Animals (PDSA – UK).
88. Captain. Courtesy of the National Mining Museum Scotland. Unknown copyright. If you have information about its copyright, please contact gayle@100horsesinhistory.com.

Chapter 7

89. Huaso. Courtesy of the Federación Ecuestre de Chile, Santiago, Chile.
90. Big Ben. Jayne Huddleston photo, EQUESPORT, Canada.
91. Flanagan. George Little/Associated Newspapers/REX.
92. King Tut. Photo by Doubleday from the collection of the National Cowgirl Museum and Hall of Fame, Fort Worth, Texas.
93. Rugged Lark. Pastel portrait by D. Fitzgerald, courtesy of Carol Harris.
94. Snowbound. Courtesy of William C. Steinkraus.
95. Steamboat. Photo by B. C. Buffum, Denver Public Library, Western History Collection, X-13685.
96. King's Pistol. Courtesy of AQHA (the American Quarter Horse Association), Amarillo, Texas.

Chapter 8

97. Pegasus. Horses and Horse-Drawn Vehicles, Dover Publications.
98. Trojan Horse. Warner Bros./Photofest.
99. Sleipnir. Public domain.
100. Lady Godiva's Horse. Dover Digital Design Source.

Footnotes

Affirmed
"I wasn't worried about": Steve Cauthen. William Leggett, "The Race Of a Lifetime," Sports Illustrated, June 19, 1978.
"He had the speed": John Veitch. Sam Ludu, "Racing Through History," https://racinghallblog.wordpress.com/2010/07/13/hall-of-fame-profile-affirmed/.
"Affirmed," National Museum of Racing and Hall of Fame, https://www.racingmuseum.org/hall-of-fame/horses.

Algonquin
"a calico or pinto": Outdoor pastimes of an American hunter, p. 356.
"When the second floor was reached": "PONY IN THE WHITE HOUSE," New York Times, April 27, 1903.
Theodore Roosevelt Birthplace National Historic Site, "The Roosevelt Pets," www.nps.gov/thrb/historyculture/the-roosevelt-pets.htm.

American Pharoah
"The third time was a charm." Victor Espinoza. Paul Volponi. Blood-Horse. June 13, 2015.
"So Who Misspelled American Pharoah?" Melissa Hoppert.
www.nytimes.com/2015/05/22/sports/american-pharoah-may-be-seeking-triple-crown-but-letter-perfect-he's-not.html.
www.komu.com/news/mid-missouri-woman-has-unique-ties-to-american-pharoah. June 4, 2015

Aristides
"fastest two minutes in sports": Origin unknown, attributed possibly to Bill Corum, Grantland Rice, Matt Winn, or Red Smith.
"all grades of society": History of the Kentucky Derby, p. 6
"that portion of the Grand Stand": Ibid.
"Garland of Roses," www.kentuckyderby.com/experience/traditions/roses.
"History of Churchill Downs," www.churchilldowns.com/about/history.
"History of the Garland of Roses," www.derbyexperiences.com/history.
"Oliver Lewis Biography," biography.jrank.org/pages/2969/Lewis-Oliver.html.
(The) "Run for the Roses," term coined in 1925 by Bill Corum, a New York sports writer, columnist, and president of Churchill Downs.
"Traditions," www.kentuckyderby.com/party/derby-info/traditions.

Babe
"Horse and Diver Fall": New York Times, July 12, 1908, p. 13.
"and when (Babe) jumps, oh, the glory of it all": Mamie Francis, unknown Pittsburgh newspaper.
"After (a) while, I will be able": Mamie Francis, The Gazette Times (Pittsburgh), June 26, 1910.
Tom Shelton, grandson of Mamie Francis (Hafley), telephone interviews.
The National Cowgirl Museum and Hall of Fame.

Battleship
"She's a lovely person": Reg Hobbs, The Grand National, p. 53.
"The American Pony": Jay Trump, p. 87.
"History," www.nationalsteeplechase.com/chasing/history/.
"The Story of Battleship," www.montpelierraces.org/history-of-montpelier/the-story-of-battleship/.
"Battleship," National Museum of Racing and Hall of Fame, https://www.racingmuseum.org/hall-of-fame/horses.

Big Ben
"I want to make sure everyone knows": Ian Millar. Beverley Smith, "Big Ben a rich winner in Spruce Meadows latest triumph," The Globe and Mail (Calgary, Alberta, Canada), Sept. 9, 1991, p. C6.
"Ben won everything": Ian Millar, www.millarbrookefarm.com/en.
For the Love of a Horse, Big Ben Park, www.bigben.ca.
Canada's Sports Hall of Fame, Calgary, Alberta, Canada, www.sportshall.ca.
"Jumper – Big Ben," Jump Canada Hall of Fame, www.equinecanada.ca/halloffame/index.

Black Beauty
"a large pleasant meadow": Black Beauty, p. 13
"No, my dear": Master Blomefield, Black Beauty, p. 77.
"Anna Sewell," www.enotes.com/topics/anna-sewell.

Black Gold
"hoof dangling as on a thread": "Black Gold Ends Career Where He Started in 1923," The New Orleans Item, Jan. 19, 1928.
"That Black Gold possessed": Ibid.
"Ode To A Splendid Horse," Fair Grounds Race Course (New Orleans) Media Guide, 1994 – 95.
"The Hall of Fame: Black Gold," The Blood-Horse, August 5, 1989.

"Black Gold," National Museum of Racing and Hall of Fame, https://www.racingmuseum.org/hall-of-fame/horses.

Black Jack
Black Jack was hardest to control "when I was supposed to be standing still": Arthur Carlson, telephone interview.
"At the time": Ibid.
"Caisson Platoon," www.oldguard.mdw.army.mil/specialty-platoons/caisson.

Blaze
"a great trampling Flemish mare": The Fair Maid of Perth, or Saint Valentine's Day, www.gutenberg.org/files/7987/7987-h/7987-h.htm#link2HCH0008. Chapter VIII, third paragraph.
"History and Characteristics of the Clydesdale Breed," Clydesdale Breeders of the U.S.A., Pecatonica, Ill., www.clydesusa.com.
Clydesdale Horse Society, Fife, Scotland, www.clydesdalehorsesociety.com.

Brigham
Brigham "understood everything": Life of Buffalo Bill, p. 157.
Buffalo Bill Historical Center, www.bbhc.org.
Special thanks to Judy Hilovsky, Managing Editor; and Leslie Baker, Director of PR and Publications; National Cowboy & Western Heritage Museum.

Bucephalus
"What an excellent horse": Alexander the Great, Great Books of the Western World, "Alexander 356 – 323 B.C.," p. 543.
"O my son": King Philip II of Macedonia, ibid.

Burmese
"It made no difference to her": Ralph Cave, telephone interview. Reproduced with permission from EQUUS Magazine.
"The shiny black mare": Ibid.
"became the perfect lady's horse": Fred Rasmussen, telephone interview, ibid..
"She was the right size": Ibid.
"Burmese was a kind": Ibid.
"Burmese, picture postcard royal mount, is dead," Times of London, July 4, 1990, p. 7.
"Trooping the Colour 2009: Her Majesty The Queen's Birthday Parade," brochure, Household Division.
"1981: Queen shot at by youth," news.bbc.co.uk/onthisday/hi/dates/stories/june/13/newsid_2512000/2512333.stm.

Buttermilk
"Buttermilk and Trigger," Ol' Waddy, Western Horseman, Sept. 1960, pp. 16-17, 91, 94.

Cannonade
"This was beautiful": Angel Cordero, Jr., "Cordero Gives Pincay $3,000 in pact," The Courier-Journal & Times, May 5, 1974, p. C5.

Captain
"I once had a sweet wee pony": Harry Lauder, "Harry Lauder as Miner," Scottish Mining website, www.scottishmining.co.uk.302.html.
"Captain's instinct": Ibid.
"When I realized": Ibid.
"A wise wee boy": Harry Lauder, "Harry Lauder – How He Was Saved By A Pit Pony," Evening News, Wellington, New Zealand, Jan. 10, 1914, p. 11. Paperspastnat.lb.govt.nz.

Champion
1907 Gene Autry Centennial 2007, The Official Website of Gene Autry, geneautry.com.
Gene Autry Entertainment, Studio City, California.
Special thanks to Maxine Hansen, executive assistant to Mrs. Gene Autry.

Cincinnati
"Lincoln spent the latter days": Ulysses S. Grant, "Grant the Equestrian," www.granthomepage.com/grantequestrian.htm.
"In horsemanship...he was noted as": CSA General James Longstreet, ibid.

Citation
"He's the greatest horse": Eddie Arcaro. James Roach, "Colt Ties Record," New York Times, June 13, 1948, Sports, pp. 1, 4.
"Citation," National Museum of Racing and Hall of Fame, https://www.racingmuseum.org/hall-of-fame/horses.

Comanche
"too weak to stand": Comanche, letter from Theodore W. Goldin to The University of Kansas Museum, Sept. 22, 1921, p. 5.
"(his) comfort": Comanche, General Orders Number Seven, issued by Col. Samuel D. Sturgis, Fort Abraham Lincoln, April 10, 1878, p. 6.
"I have seen": Letter from Goldin to The University of Kansas Museum, Sept. 22, 1921, p. 6.
John A. Doerner, Chief Historian, Little Bighorn Battlefield National Monument, Mont., telephone interview.

Copenhagen
"There may have been faster horses": Duke of Wellington, Apsley House, Hyde Park Corner, London, England.
"The Battle of Waterloo," World Book INK, blog.worldbook.com/tag/the-battle-of-waterloo/.

Creation's King
"the high stepping aristocrat of the show ring": American Hackney Horse Society, Hackneysociety.com.

"ultimate driving machine": "History of the Hackney," Hackneysociety.com/history.
"Golden Age of Driving," ibid.

Dan Patch
"Dan Patch at $60,000": Marion W. Savage. Robert Warn, "The Story of Marion Savage & Dan Patch," Golden Nugget, Dec. 29, 1971.
"Dan Patch Birth Centennial 1896 – 1996," Dan Patch Newsletter: A publication of the Dan Patch Historical Society, Savage, Minn.
U.S. Trotting Association, www.trotting.com.

Daredevil and Gunpowder
"the very witching time of night": "The Legend of Sleepy Hollow," first published in The Sketch Book of Geoffrey Crayon, Gent., (1820), p. 80.
"In the dark shadow": Ibid., p. 86.

Dawndee
Kendra Carlson, telephone interview, Appaloosa Horse Club, Moscow, Idaho, www.appaloosa.com/association.

Devon Loch
"Never before in the National": Sport of Queens, p. 220.
"The tremendous noise": Ibid., p. 229.

Eclipse
"Eclipse first, the rest nowhere": Dennis O'Kelly, "Father of Race Horses," Sports Illustrated, Aug 22, 1955.
"Heart of the Matter," Marianna Haun, The Quarter Racing Journal, June 1998.
"Eclipse," Anne Peters, www.tbheritage.com/Portraits/Eclipse.html.

Elijah
"Haylift Is Only Comfort," The Denver Post, April 8, 1956.
"Children Promise Home for Elijah," Rocky Mountain News, April 10, 1956, p. 8.
"Post Climbers Find Elijah's," George McWilliams, The Denver Post, April 13, 1956, p. 1.
"Haylift Goes on as New Snow Covers Elijah's Lofty Perch," The Denver Post, April 17, 1956.
"he'll work his way down": Bill Turner, The Denver Post, April 12, 1956.
Elijah plaque, National Cowboy & Western Heritage Museum.
Jody Grieb, interview.
Buck Turner, Bill Turner's son, interview.

Eohippus
"dawn horse": Encyclopedia Britannica. www.britannica.com/EBchecked/topic/152990/dawn-horse.
"Wild Horses, An American Romance," PBS, http://net.unl.edu/artsFeat/wildhorses.
International Museum of the Horse, Kentucky Horse Park, Lexington, Ky.

Favory Africa
"Equestrian art": The Complete Training of Horse and Rider in the Principles of Classical Horsemanship, p. 20.
"The 2nd Cavalry," www.lipizzaner.com/2ndcavalry.asp.
United States Lipizzan Federation, Las Vegas, Nev., www.uslipizzan.org.

Flanagan
"His brave heart": Pat Smythe, Flanagan My Friend, p. 28.
"Flanagan, with his easy temperament": Ibid., p. 29.

Flicka
"He hadn't had to choose": My Friend Flicka, p. 132.

Gaines' Denmark 61
"John Hunt Morgan," enwikipedia.org/wiki/John_Hunt_Morgan.
"The Saddlebred Denmark," American Saddlebred Museum, www.asbmuseum.org.
Special thanks to Kim Skipton, Curator, American Saddlebred Museum.

Gallant Man
"I stood up for an instant": Willie Shoemaker. Johnny Carrico, "Erb Not Mad by Near-Miss Of Derby Win," The Courier-Journal, May 5, 1957, Section 2, p. 1.

Goliath
Melissa Heaver, Registrar/Research Director, telephone interviews, The Fire Museum of Maryland, www.firemuseummd.org.

Hambletonian 10
David Carr, telephone interview, U.S. Trotting Association (USTA), Columbus, Ohio, www.ustrotting.com.
Paul Wilder, telephone interviews, Harness Racing Museum & Hall Fame, www.harnessmuseum.com.
"Hambletonian," Harness Racing Museum & Hall of Fame, www.harnessmuseum.com/pages/main-home-page-info/hambopage.htm.

His Honour, a Houyhnhnm
"the perfection of nature": Gulliver's Travels, p. 236.

"said the thing which was not": Ibid.
"naturally disposed to every virtue": Ibid., p. 272.

Huaso
"As I approached the jump": Captain Larraguibel Morales, "Chilean Equitation," Santiago (Chile) Chamber of Commerce.
"From my end": Ibid.
"Huaso – A Leap Into History," Gayle Stewart, EQUUS Magazine, June 2001, pp. 114-119.

Jay Trump
"like a cavalry charge": Tommy Smith, Jay Trump, A Steeplechasing Saga, p. 118.
"Jay Trump had never jumped": Ibid., p. 120.
"Keep inside": Fred Winter, recalled by Tommy Smith, ibid., p. 116.
Let "Jay Trump": Ibid.
"Jay Trump," National Museum of Racing and Hall of Fame, www.racingmuseum.org/hall-of-fame/horses.

Joey
"We were back among the fearful noise": Joey, War Horse, pp. 87, 88.

Justify
"He's so gifted." Mike Smith. Melissa Hoppert, "Simply Perfect: Justify Wins the Triple Crown." www.nytimes.com/ 2018/06/09/sports/Belmont-stakes-justify.html.
"Just listening to the crowd": Bob Baffert, Steve Haskin, "At Last," Blood-Horse, June 13, 2015, p. 39.

Justin Morgan
"a horse that was right every way": Solomon Yurann. Morgan Horses, p. 48.
"A horse with a heritage," "The Year of the Morgan," brochure, pp. 6, 7. American Morgan Horse Association, Shelburne, Vt., www.morganhorse.com.
"Justin Morgan," "The Morgan Mile Trotting Races," Vermont Morgan Horse Association, Inc., www.morganmile.com/justin.html.
"Life and Times of Figure," Elizabeth A. Curler, National Museum of the Morgan Horse, 1998, nmmh.tripod.com/figure.html.

King Tut
"Bonnie sat right up there": Reba Perry Blakely, "Bonnie Gray – A Gifted Show Woman," World of Rodeo and Western Heritage, June 25, 1978.
"Bonnie Gray Harris," National Cowgirl Museum and Hall of Fame, www.cowgirl.net/HallofFameHonorees/Harris.Bonnie.html.
"Frontier Days Trick Riding II – Wyoming Tales and Trails," www.wyomingtalesandtrails.com/frontierdays6.html.
Special thanks to Bethany Dodson, Research and Education Manager, National Cowgirl Museum and Hall of Fame.

King's Pistol
"short-legged, pot-bellied": Jim Calhoun. Phil Livingston, Legends, Volume 2, p. 106.
"drove a yearling out of the bunch": Ibid., p. 108.
"If a horse is smart": Ibid.
Alan Gold, telephone interviews, National Cutting Horse Association, Fort Worth, Tex., www.nchacutting.com.
Special thanks to Fran Smith, Western Horseman Book Publishing Director.

Lady Godiva's Horse
Colin T. Clarkson, email interview, University of Cambridge, Cambridge, England.
"Lady Godiva," www.biography.com/people/lady-godiva.

Lady Suffolk
"The Old Gray Mare," song, author unknown, www.fresnostate.edu/folklore/ballads/R271.html.
"equivalent of breaking the sound barrier": The Complete Book of Harness Racing, p. 17.
"the trotting sport came up": Ibid.
"The First 2:30 Trotter," John Hervey, Hoof Beats, Jan. 1945.
Paul Wilder, Harness Racing Museum & Hall of Fame, telephone interviews.
Special thanks to John M. Zak, Currier and Ives historian, Farmingdale, N.Y.

Little Sorrel
"as easy as the rocking of a cradle": Stonewall Jackson, Life and Times of General Thomas J. Jackson (Stonewall Jackson), p. 171.
Little Sorrel "seemed absolutely indefatigable": Mary Anna Jackson, ibid.
"Battle of Chancellorsville," www.civilwar.org/battlefields/chancellorsville/chancellorsville-history-articles/10-facts-about-html.
"Blame the Full Moon for Stonewall Jackson's Death," Lee Rannals, redOrbit.com, www.civilwarfamily.us/2013/blame-the-full-moon-for-stonewall-jacksons-death.html.
"Lee's Greatest Victory," "Battle of Chancellorsville History," www.nps.gov/frsp/historyculture/cvillehistory.htm.

Macaroni
John F. Kennedy Presidential Library and Museum, www.jfklibrary.org.
Lyndon Baines Johnson Presidential Library, www.lbjlibrary.org.

Man o' War
"He's got everything a horse ought to have": Will Harbut. There are several versions of this quotation recited by Will Harbut when presenting Man o' War to visitors. Harbut's son, Tom, confirmed them to Bill Cooke, Director, International Museum of the Horse, Kentucky Horse Park.
"I looked back several times": Clarence Kummer, "MAN O'WAR VICTOR OVER SIR BARTON BY SEVEN LENGTHS," New York Times, Oct. 13, 1920.

"He broke all the records": K. L. Jones, "Thoroughbred Bloodlines – Twentieth Century Stallions," www.bloodlines.net/TB/Bios2/Bios-M/ManOWar.htm.
"Big Red sets record at Belmont Stakes," June 12, 1920, www.history/com/this-day-in-history/big-red-sets-record-at-belmont-stakes.
"Man o' War, Turf King of America, Succumbs at 30 of Heart Attack," New York Times, Nov. 2, 1947.
"Man o War," National Museum of Racing Hall of Fame, https://www.racingmuseum.org/hall-of-fame/horses.

Man o' War and Secretariat
"Both defied comparison": Joe Hirsch, "The Century's Two Greatest Horses," Daily Racing Form, Oct. 6, 1989.

Manitou
"Black care rarely": Ranch Life and The Hunting-Trail, p. 59.
"My own hunting-horse": Hunting Trips of a Ranchman, p. 41.
"Manitou is a treasure": Ibid, p. 42.
"Theodore Roosevelt Timeline," National Park Service, www.nps.gov/thro/historyculture/theodoreroosevelt-timeline.htm.

Marengo
"A horse has memory": Napoleon Bonaparte, Napoleon at St. Helena, p. 183.
"The Battle of Waterloo 1815 the most famous of all Napoleon battles," www.napoleon-battles.com.

Merrylegs
"Why, I am as careful": Merrylegs, Black Beauty, p. 55.
"Boys, you see": Ibid., p. 56.
"I can tell you": Ibid., p. 58.

Mister Ed
"Ed handled his part": Mister Ed and Me, p. 185.
"Leo Durocher Meets Mister Ed," Season 4, Episode 1, first aired Sept. 29, 1963, Filmways Television and MGM Television.
"The 100 Greatest Episodes of All Time," TV Guide, June 28, 1997.

Misty of Chincoteague
"When I was in the woods there": Paul Beebe, Misty of Chincoteague, p. 91.

Mr. Butler
"When you are six": Rhett Butler, Gone With The Wind, p. 990.
"They are, too": Bonnie Blue Butler, ibid.
"No, you must wait": Rhett Butler, ibid.

Occident
"the first shadowy and indistinct picture": Muybridge letter. Time Stands Still. Muybridge and the Instantaneous Photography Movement, p. 135.
"Occident, Leland Stanford's horse, first movie star," John Sanford, Stanford Report, Sept. 5, 2001, news.stanford.edu/news/2001/september5/filmstudiessidebar-95.html.

Old Billy
"an extremely vicious": Mr. W. Johnson. Old Billy: 1760 – 1822. The world's oldest horse, p. 7.
"very savagely": Ibid.

Old Bob
"A splendid old horse": Unknown attribution, Twenty Days, p. 264.

Olga
"PDSA Dickin Medal Horses": Pdsa.org.uk/about-us/animal-bravery-awards/pdsa-dickin-medal.

Paul Revere's Horse
"I set off upon a very good horse": Revere letter to Jeremy Belknap, Paul Revere's Three Accounts of His Famous Ride, Boston: Massachusetts Historical Society, 2000.
"I got a Horse of Deacon Larkin": Ibid.
"the moon shone bright": Paul Revere, The Deposition: Corrected Copy. Ibid.
"I turned my horse short": Ibid.
"In Medford": Revere letter to Belknap, ibid.
"The regulars are coming out": William Munroe. Edmund Morgan, "The Making of Paul Revere," ibid.
"slapping his leather breeches": H. N. H., William Dawes's granddaughter. William Dawes and His Ride With Paul Revere, p. 37.
"thrown to the ground": M. M. G., William Dawes's daughter. Ibid., p. 35.
"Halloo, my boys!": William Dawes. H. N. H., ibid., p. 37.
"Samuel (Larkin)...born Oct. 22, 1701; died Oct. 8, 1784, aged 83; he was a chairmaker, then a fisherman and had horses and a stable. He was the owner of 'Brown Beauty,' the mare of Paul Revere's ride made famous by the Longfellow poem. The mare was loaned at the request of Samuel's son, deacon John Larkin, and was never returned to the owner." Larkin Family Genealogy, 1930, The Paul Revere House.
"The Real Story of Paul Revere's Ride," The Paul Revere House, http://www.paulreverehouse.org/ride/real.html.
Patrick M. Leehey, Research Director, The Paul Revere House, telephone interviews.

Pegasus

"Asleep? Nay, wake": Athena, Mythology, p. 186.
"Bellerophon," www.greekmythology.com/Myths/Heroes/Bellerophon/bellerophon.html.

Phar Lap
"He was an angel": Harry Telford, "The Legend," Museum Victoria, Australia, museumvictoria.com.au/pharlap/.
"Melbourne Cup," www.australia.gov.au/about-australia-story/melbourne-cup.
"Phar Lap," Liz Martiniak, http://wwwtbheritage.com/Portraits/Pharlap.html.

Pluto
"And the Lipizzaner!": The White Stallions of Vienna, introduction.
"Lipizzan Dynasties," Lipizzan International Federation, www.lipizzan.com/lipizzandynasties.html.
"Spanish Riding School, Vienna," brochure, Spanish Riding School.

Red Rum
"He's coming up to the line": Sir Peter O'Sullevan, race call excerpt (April 2, 1977). Reproduced by permission of the BBC, www.bbc.co.uk.
The "world's greatest steeplechase": www.grandnational.net/history.htm.
"Ginger McCain and Red Rum – History of the Grand National," www.aintree.co.uk/pages/history-of-the-grand-national-red-rum/.
"Grand National Special 2012: Tribute to Ginger McCain – Red Rum 1977," Chris Wright, Liverpool Echo, April 2, 2012. www.liverpoolecho.co.uk/sport/horse-racing/grand-national-special-20120-tribute-3346300.
Special thanks to Sir O'Sullevan.

Rocinante
"tilting at windmills," www.phrases.org.uk/meanings/tilting-at-windmills.html.

Rugged Lark
"He was a superstar": Carol Harris, Rugged Lark's breeder and owner, Bo-Bett Farm, Reddick, Fla., email interviews.
"Rugged Lark," Richard Chamberlain, The Quarter Horse Journal, July 29, 2011, Americashorsedaily.com/rugged-lark/.

Ruthless
"the following day": National Museum of Racing and Hall of Fame, https://www.racingmuseum.org/hall-of-fame/horses.

Samson
Sleeping Beauty, Walt Disney Pictures, 1959, DVD.

Seabiscuit
"The Admiral looked Seabiscuit": Grantland Rice, "Seabiscuit Tops Admiral By Three Lengths Before Pimlico Crowd of 40,000," The Baltimore Sun, Nov. 2, 1938, pp. 1, 15.
"A Horse You Had to Like," Red Smith, New York Herald Tribune, May 20, 1947.
"Red Pollard," www.pbs.org/wgbh/americanexperience/features/biography/seabiscuit-biography-red-pollard/
"Seabiscuit," National Museum of Racing and Hall of Fame, https://racingmuseum.org/hall-of-fame/horses.
"1938 Pimlico Special," Horse Racing Nation, www.horseracingnation.com/race/PIM_19381101_Race_1_Allow.
"1940 Santa Anita Handicap," Horse Racing Nation, www.horseracingnation.com/race/1940_Santa_Anita_Handicap.

Seattle Slew
"A very special horse": Karen Taylor. John B. Sault, "Story of Seattle Slew lives on," Seattle Times, May 4, 2007.
"If Seattle was human": Angel Cordero. Andrew Beyer, "Seattle Slew: Stallion's champion bloodlines flow on," Austin American-Statesman from The Washington Post, May 8, 2012.
"Seattle Slew," National Museum of Racing and Hall of Fame, https://www.racingmuseum.org/hall-of-fame/horses.

Secretariat
"He looked like a Rolls-Royce": Chic Lang, Pimlico Race Course announcer. Ron Flatter, "Secretariat remains No. 1 name in racing," espn.go.com/classic/biography/s/Secretariat.html.
"This red horse": Penny Chenery, ibid.
"Secretariat," National Museum of Racing and Hall of Fame, https://www.racingmuseum.org/hall-of-fame/horses.

Sergeant Reckless
"take cover while on the front lines": Nancy Lee White Hoffman, "Sgt. Reckless: Combat Veteran," Nov. 1992, www.mca-marines/org/leatherneck-sgt-reckless-combat-veteran.
"It was in the battle": Unknown attribution, Reckless – Pride of the Marines, p. 209.
"The Four-Legged Marine in Korea," Corporal Lesli Coakley, Around the Corps, Department of the Navy, History and Museums, Camp Pendleton, Calif., Sept. 1991, p. 23.

Shirayuki
Imperial Household Agency Archives, Tokyo, Japan.

Siete Leguas
"The bullet passed": Centaur of the North, p. 174.

Silver
"So they brought back Silver number one": I Was That Masked Man, p. 159.

Sir Barton

"During the last eighth": "Sir Barton Easily Wins the Belmont," New York Times, June 12, 1919.
"Sir Barton," Canadian Racing Hall of Fame, www.canadianracinghalloffame.com
"Sir Barton. The First Triple Crown Winner," Jenny Kellner, www.belmontstakes.com/history/sirbarton.aspx.

Sleipnir
"And he will fare": The Poems of Matthew Arnold, first published in 1855, www.bartleby.com/254/82.html.

Smuggler
"Fastest Trotting Stallion in the United States": Yankee Weathervanes, p. 171.

Snowbound
"Nothing ever fazed him": William C. Steinkraus, "My Memories of Snowbound," www.chronofhorse.com, Jan. 19, 2009.
"We never tried to see": Ibid.
"With all his faults": Barbara Worth Oakford, "Snowbound," Great Horses of Our Time, p. 500.
William C. Steinkraus, telephone interview.

Snowman
"Look, Daddy": Harriet de Leyer, from The Eighty-Dollar Champion, p. 13.
"As the horse cleared": Alice Higgins, "German Cliffhanger," Sports Illustrated, Nov. 24, 1958. Harry de Leyer, telephone interviews.

Special Effort
"Special Effort," www.aqha.com/Foundation/Museum/Hall-of-Fame/Horses/S/Special-Effort.aspx.

Steamboat
"Steamboat – One of the Toughest Broncs in History of West," R. H. "Bob" Burns and A. S. "Bud" Gillespie, Hoofs and Horns, March 1952.
Steamboat plaque, National Cowboy & Western Heritage Museum.

Survivor
"Preakness Stakes History," www.thoroughbredtimes.com/triple-crown/about-the-preakness-stakes.aspx.

Sylph
"Hardly will the cloud of dust": St. Joseph Mayor Jeff Thompson, www.ci.st-joseph.mo.us//history/mayors_thompson.cfm.
Commemorative program, Pony Express National Memorial Grand Opening, April 3, 1993.
"History," Pony Express National Museum, ponyexpress.org.
Brenda Eaves and Michelle Mooney, Pony Express National Museum, telephone interviews.

Teddy
"A man that don't love": Will Rogers, Weekly Articles #88, Will Rogers Memorial Museums, www.willrogers.com.
"I have always said": Ibid., Weekly Articles #392.
"Teddy could do on a slick stage": Ibid., Weekly Articles #649.
"all I know is just": Ibid., Weekly Articles #392.
Steve Gragert, Executive Director, Will Rogers Memorial Museums, email interview.

Tennessee Stud
"He raised horses": Jimmie Driftwood. Sing Your Heart Out, Country Boy, pp. 410, 411.
"Tennessee Stud," Max Brantley and Stephen Koch, Arkansas Times, March 17, 2005, www.arktimes.com/arkansas/tennessee-stud/Content?oid = 862932.

The Black Stallion
"Alec flung his arms:" The Black Stallion, p. 31.
"He saved my life": Alec Ramsay, ibid., p. 39.

The Byerley Turk
"Turkes or Asian Horses": John Evelyn's Diary, 1684, Thoroughbred Racing Stock and Its Ancestors, p. 173.
"They trotted like does": Ibid., pp. 173-174.
"the best racehorse": The Byerley Turk, p. 29.
"Byerley's Treasure": The Arabian Horse, p. 105.
"Beware a Base Breed: Notes Toward a Revisionist History of the Thoroughbred Racehorse," Dr. Richard Nash, Professor of English, Indiana University.
"The Byerley Turk," Anne Peters, Thoroughbred Heritage Portraits, www.bloodlines.net/TB/Bios/ByerleyTurk.html.
Special thanks to Clare Oglesby, owner, Goldsborough Hall, North Yorkshire, England.

The Darley Arabian
"he has a blaze": Thomas Darley in letter to his brother Richard, Dec. 21, 1703. Peter Darley, "The Darley Arabian," www.genuki.org.uk/big/eng/YKS/Misc/Descriptions/NRY/ButtercrambeArabian.html.
"I believe he will not be much disliked": Ibid.

The Godolphin Arabian
"a horse of incomparable beauty": Vicomte de Manty, The Godolphin Arabian, p. 2.
"the best racehorse": The Godolphin Arabian, p. 6.
"The Godolphin Arabian," Anne Peters, Thoroughbred Heritage Portraits, http://www.tbheritage.com/Portraits/GodolphinArabian.html.

The Maltese Cat

"The Maltese Cat knew": "The Maltese Cat," from short-story collection The Day's Work.

The Piebald

"Oh, God, give me horses": Velvet Brown, National Velvet, p. 17.

The Trojan Horse

"Trust not their presents": Laocoon, the priest. Virgil, The Aeneid, Book II, a Latin epic poem written between 29 BC and 19 BC.
"Beware of Greeks": en.wikipedia.org/wiki/List_of_proverbial_phrases.
"The Fall of Troy," Ancienthistory.about.com/library/bl/bl_text_bulfinch_1.htm. Chapter 28.

Traveller

"As he passed": "Longstreet: From Manassas to Appomattox," The War Times Journal, www.wtj.com/archives/longstreet/.
"always acknowledged the cheers": Unknown attribution, R. E. Lee., Vol. IV, p. 147.
"(Traveller) was bespattered": Ibid., p. 161.
"Have patience with Traveller": Robert E. Lee, ibid., p. 308.
"How is Traveller?": Robert E. Lee, Traveller – General Robert E. Lee's Horse, brochure, Washington and Lee University, Lexington, Va.
Patrick Schroeder, Historian, Appomattox Court House National Historical Park, telephone interviews.

Trigger

"If there hadn't been a Trigger": Roy Rogers, The Roy Rogers Book, p. 73.
"the ham in that horse": Roy Rogers. H. Allen Smith, "King of the Cowboys," Life, July 12, 1943, p. 52.
"All those years": Roy Rogers, The Roy Rogers Book, p. 72.
"B-Western Horses," Raymond E. White, Western Horseman, June 2001, p. 54-59.
Special thanks to Roy Rogers, Jr.

Vic

John A. Doerner, Chief Historian, Little Bighorn Battlefield National Monument, telephone interview.
Douglas C. McChristian, Chief Historian, ibid., letter.

Wimpy P-1

"there was a sizable crowd": Frank Reeves, Fort Worth Star-Telegram, March 14, 1941, p. 20.
"They Called Him Wimpy," Jim Jennings, America's Horse, Nov./Dec. 2002, American Quarter Horse Association, Amarillo, Tex.
Special thanks to Lisa Neely, Archivist, King Ranch©.

Winchester

"an animal of great intelligence": Gen. Philip Sheridan, www.civilwar.si.edu/cavalry_winchester_html.
"12 miles distant": "The Battle of Cedar Creek," www.ccbf.us/?page_id-8.

Books

American Morgan Horse Association, Shelburne, Vt., "A horse with a heritage," *The Year of the Morgan*.

Archer, Rosemary. *The Arabian Horse*. London: J. A. Allen & Co., Ltd., 1991.

Associated Press. *The Torch is Passed: The Associated Press Story of the Death of a President*. New York: Associated Press, 1963.

Bagnold, Enid. *National Velvet*. New York: William Morrow and Co., Inc., 1949.

Birkenhead, Lord. *Rudyard Kipling*. New York: Random House, 1978.

Bowen, Edward L. *At The Wire, Horse Racing's Greatest Moments*. Lexington, Ky.: Eclipse Press, The Blood-Horse, Inc., 2001.

Cervantes, Miguel de. *The Adventures of the Don Quixote de la Mancha*. New York: Modern Library, Random House Publishing Group, 2001. Translated from Spanish by Tobias Smollett.

Cody, William F. "Buffalo Bill." *Life of Buffalo Bill, an autobiography*. Hartford: Frank E. Bliss, 1879.

Crossley-Holland, Kevin. *The Norse Myths*. New York: Pantheon Books, 1980.

Curling, Bill & Clive Graham. *The Grand National. An Illustrated History of the Greatest Steeplechase in the World*. New York: Winchester Press, 1972.

Daly, Kathleen N. *Greek and Roman Mythology A to Z: A Young Reader's Companion*. New York: Facts On File, Inc., 1992.

Dary, David. *Comanche*. The University of Kansas, Museum of Natural History, Lawrence, Kansas, 1976.

D'aulaires, Edgar Parin and Ingri. *Book of Greek Myths*. New York: Bantam Doubleday Dell Publishing Group, Inc., 1962.

Edwards, Peter; Karl Enenkel and Elspeth Graham, editors. *The Horse as Cultural Icon*. Boston: Brill Press, 2011.

Farley, Walter. *The Black Stallion*. New York: Random House, 1941.

Francis, Dick. *The Sport of Queens*. New York: Penzler Books, 1957.

Friddell, Claudia. *Goliath: Hero of the Great Baltimore Fire*. Ann Arbor, Mich.: Sleeping Bear Press, 2010.

Forbes, Esther. *Paul Revere and the World He Lived In*. Boston: Houghton-Mifflin. 1942, 1969.

Freeman, Douglas Southall. *R. E. Lee, A Biography*. New York: Charles Scribner's Sons, 1935.

Frost, Lawrence. A. *General Custer's Thoroughbreds*. Mattituck, New York: J. M. Carroll & Co., 1986.

Geer, Andrew. *Reckless, Pride of the Marines*. New York: E. P. Dutton and Co., 1955.

Griffiths, Ralph A. "Lady Godiva." *The World Book Encyclopedia*. Chicago: World Book. Inc., 1996.

Guerber, H. A. *The Norsemen. Myths and Legends Series*. New York: Avenel Books, 1986.

Hamilton, Edith. *Mythology*. New York, Boston: Little, Brown and Company, 1942.

Haralambos, K. M. *The Byerley Turk. Three centuries of the tail male racing lines*. London: Threshold Books, 1990.

Henry, Marguerite. *Misty of Chincoteague*. New York: Aladdin Paperbacks, 1947.

Hervey, John. *The American Trotter*. New York: Coward-McCann, Inc., 1947.

Holland, Henry W. *William Dawes and His Ride With Paul Revere*. Boston: John Wilson and Son, 1878.

Horstman, Dorothy. *Sing Your Heart Out, Country Boy*. Nashville: Country Music Foundation Press, Third Edition, 1986.

Irving, Washington. *The Sketch Book of Geoffrey Crayon, Gent*. "The Legend of Sleepy Hollow." New York: C. S. Van Winkle, 1819-1820.

Jackson, Mary Anna. *Life and Letters of General Thomas J. Jackson (Stonewall Jackson)*. Originally published: New York: Harper & Brothers, 1892.

Kaye, Myrna. *Yankee Weathervanes*. New York: E. P. Dutton and Co., 1975.

Kipling, Rudyard. *The Day's Work, written in 1898*. London: Macmillan & Company, 1936. www.readbooksonline.net/readOnline/2409.

Kunhardt, Dorothy Meserve, and Philip B. Kunhardt, Jr. *Twenty Days*. New York: Harper and Row, 1965.

Leehey, Patrick M., Coordinator of Research, The Paul Revere House. *What was the Name of Paul Revere's Horse?* Boston: Paul Revere Memorial Association, 1997.

Letts, Elizabeth. *The Eighty-Dollar Champion*. New York: Ballantine Books, 2011.

Machado, Manuel A., Jr. *Centaur of the North*. Austin, Tex.: Eakin Press, 1988.

McLynn, Frank. *Villa and Zapata: A History of the Mexican Revolution*. New York: Carroll and Graf, 2000.

Miller, D. H. *Custer's Fall – The Indian Side of the Story*. New York: Duell, Sloan and Pierce, 1957.

Milner, Mordaunt. *The Godolphin Arabian, the Story of the Matchem Line*. London: J. A. Allen & Co., Ltd., 1990.

Mitchell, Margaret. *Gone With The Wind*. New York: Macmillan Company, 1944.

Moore, Clayton, with Frank Thompson. *I Was That Masked Man*. Dallas: Taylor Publishing Co., 1996.

Morpurgo, Michael. *War Horse*. New York: Scholastic, Inc., 2007.

Nack, William. *Secretariat, The Making of a Champion*. Cambridge, Mass.: Da Capo Press, 1975, 2002.

O'Connor, John L. *History of the Kentucky Derby, 1875 – 1921*. New York: Rider Press Co., 1921.

O'Hara, Mary. *My Friend Flicka*. Philadelphia, New York: J. B. Lippincott Company, 1941.

O'Meara, Barry. *Napoleon at St. Helena*. New York: Scribner and Welford, Vol. 1, 1889.

Paul Revere's Three Accounts of His Famous Ride. Boston: Massachusetts Historical Society, 2000.

Pines, Philip A. *The Complete Book of Harness Racing*. New York: Arco Publishing, Fourth Edition, 1982.

_____and Evelyn Slobody and Lawrence Slobody, editors. *Trotting – A Pageant of Horse Prints*. Benson Press, 1984.

Pittenger, Peggy Jett. *Morgan Horses*. New York: Arco (no date).

Plutarch. "Alexander." *Great Books of the Western World*. Encyclopedia Britannica, Inc., Vol. 14, Second Edition, 1990.

Podhajsky, Alois. T*he Complete Training of Horse and Rider in the Principles of Classical Horsemanship*. Garden City, NY: Doubleday and Company, Inc., 1967.

_____*The White Stallions of Vienna*. New York: E. P. Dutton & Co., 1963.

Pollard, Jack. *Australian Horse Racing*. North Ryde, N.S.W.: Angus and Robertson, 1988.

Prodger, Phillip, Dr. *Time Stands Still. Muybridge and the Instantaneous Photography Movement*. New York: Oxford University Press, in association with the Iris and B. Gerald Cantor Center for Visual Arts at Stanford University, 2003.

Rogers, Betty. *Will Rogers. His Wife's Story*. Norman, Okla.: University of Oklahoma Press, 1941.

Roosevelt, Theodore. *Hunting Trips of a Ranchman*. Volume 1. New York and London: G. P. Putnam's Son, 1885.

_____*Outdoor pastimes of an American hunter*. New York: Charles Scribner's Sons, 1905.

_____*Ranch Life and the Hunting-Trail*. New York: St. Martin's Press, 1985. (First published: New York: Century, 1888.)

Ropes, John Codman. *The Campaign of Waterloo – A Military History*. New York: Scribner's, 1893.

Rothel, David. *Who Was That Masked Man? Story of the Lone Ranger*. New York: A. S. Barnes, 1977.

_____*The Roy Rogers Book*. Madison, N.C.: Empire Publishing Incorporated, 1987.

Seyd, Edmund L. *Old Billy: 1760 – 1822. The world's oldest horse*. Manchester Museum Publications, The University of Manchester, 1973.

Scott, Sir Walter. *The Fair Maid of Perth, or Saint Valentine's Day*. London and New York: George Routledge & Son, 1880.

Sewell, Anna. *Black Beauty*. Racine, Wis.: Whitman Publishing Co., 1955.

Something About the Author, Vol. 24. "Mary O'Hara Alsop." Gale Research Company, 1981.

Smythe, Pat. *Flanagan My Friend*. London: Cassell & Company, Ltd., 1963.

Spaeth, Sigmund Gottfried. *A History of Popular Music in America*. New York: Random House, 1948.

Spring, Agnes Wright. *Buffalo Bill and His Horses*. Denver: Bradford-Robinson Printing Co., 1968.

Stoneridge, M. A. *Great Horses of Our Time*. New York: Doubleday & Co., 1972.

Swift, Jonathan. *Gulliver's Travels. A Voyage to the Country of the Houyhnhnms*, Part IV. New York: Barnes and Noble Books, 2003. (First published: London: Benjamin Motte, 1726.)

Trooping the Colour 2009 – Her Majesty The Queen's Birthday Parade. London: Household Division, Press Office.

TV Guide Book of Lists. Philadelphia: Running Press, 2007.

Wentworth, Lady (Judith Anne Dorothea Blunt-Lytton). "Alexander's Charger," "The Byerley Turk," "The Darley Arabian." *THOROUGHBRED RACING STOCK AND ITS ANCESTORS*. New York: The Dial Press, 1938.

Western Horseman, Inc. *Legends*: Volume 2. Colorado Springs, Colo., 1994.

Winants, Peter. *Jay Trump. A Steeplechasing Saga*. Baltimore: Winants Bros. Inc., 1966.

Woolfe, Raymond G., Jr. *Secretariat*. Lanham, Md.: Derrydale Press, 1974, 1981, 2010.

World Book Encyclopedia. "Greece, Ancient." John Harvey Kent. Chicago: Field Enterprises Educational Corporation, 1962.

Young, Alan, and Bill Burt. *Mister Ed and Me*. New York: St. Martin's Press, 1995.

About the Author

Gayle Stewart is an award-winning author who has written about all things horses for thirty years. Her horse stories have been published in *Chicken Soup for the Horse Lover's Soul* (Vol. 1), *EQUUS*, *Oklahoma Today*, *Persimmon Hill*, the Dallas *Morning News*, the *Daily Oklahoman*, and the Kansas City *Star*, among others. She is a regular contributor to Horse Radio Network's *Stable Scoop* show and won a Pegasus Award from the United States Equestrian Federation. She and her husband, Rob, have a grown son and live in the beautiful Texas Hill Country.

Contact Gayle at gayle@100horsesinhistory.com and www.100horsesinhistory.com.